Global Competitiveness and Inno

Global Competitiveness and Innovation

An Agent-Centred Perspective

Gordon L. Clark
University of Oxford
UK

and

Paul Tracey
University of Cambridge
UK

First published 2004 by
PALGRAVE MACMILLAN
Houndmills, Basingstoke, Hampshire RG21 6XS and
175 Fifth Avenue, New York, N. Y. 10010
Companies and representatives throughout the world

PALGRAVE MACMILLAN is the global academic imprint of the Palgrave Macmillan division of St. Martin's Press, LLC and of Palgrave Macmillan Ltd. Macmillan® is a registered trademark in the United States, United Kingdom and other countries. Palgrave is a registered trademark in the European Union and other countries.

ISBN 1–4039–1889–9 hardback
ISBN 1–4039–3263–8 paperback

This book is printed on paper suitable for recycling and made from fully managed and sustained forest sources.

A catalogue record for this book is available from the British Library.

Library of Congress Cataloging-in-Publication Data

Clark, Gordon L.
    Global competitiveness and innovation: an agent-centred perspective/ Gordon L. Clark and Paul Tracey.
        p. cm.
    Includes bibliographical references and index.
    ISBN 1–4039–1889–9 (cloth) – ISBN 1–4039–3263–8 (paper)
        1. Competition, International. 2. Competition. 3. International economic relations. 4. Globalization. I. Tracey, Paul, 1974– II. Title.
HF1414.C58 2004
337–dc22   2003062248

10   9   8   7   6   5   4   3   2   1
13   12   11   10   09   08   07   06   05   04

Printed and bound in Great Britain by
Antony Rowe Ltd, Chippenham and Eastbourne

For Bryan and Lesley Clark
and
Jim and Janice Tracey

Contents

List of Table and Figures

Preface

Inspiration for this book came from a large, multi-year EU sponsored project on the global and European competitiveness of small and medium size firms in labour intensive industries located in non-metropolitan regions of southern and western Europe. We pay due regard to our sponsors and partners in the Acknowledgements following this Preface. At this juncture it is sufficient to note that these kinds of projects can be wonderful learning experiences, being projects of intensive collaboration and research while combining the talents of scholars from across Europe and across a number of disciplines. This was the case in our project, although we recognise that not all such projects are blessed in this way. Papers and reports from the project, as well as the Final Report can be found on the following web sites (Oxford University) www.geog. ox.ac.uk (European Commission) www.cordis.lu/fp5/

As we began the project, wrestling with issues such as the theory and methodology of comparative economic research, we came to appreciate the variety of skills and perspectives we each brought to the project. In particular, the co-ordination team brought together Gordon L. Clark (an economic geographer with extensive research and policy-related experience in North America and North east Asia), Paul Tracey (a management researcher with experience in UK small firms and entrepreneurship), and Helen Lawton Smith (an economic geographer with a great deal of research experience in UK and European innovation studies, and urban and regional development). Over time we developed a dual-track organisation and structure; on one hand, leading the empirical project as set-out in the initial proposal while, on the other hand, developing our own perspective on the issue of comparative competitiveness in the context of global and European economic integration.

Here, the goal of this book is to articulate our analytical perspective on competitiveness relevant to regional economic development. In doing so, we are mindful of the enormous pressures being brought to bear on European communities and industries by global economic competition. Our own case studies and those of our partners in the project have convinced us that no region, no industry and no firm can claim an isolated, privileged or unassailable place in the global economy. Even those firms and regional complexes that have thrived over the past few decades are subject to the competitive forces of firms located in far-flung newly industrialising economies. Most significantly, many European and North American firms and industries are very vulnerable to price and quality competition in their core markets. Competitive and strategic responses to these corrosive forces are at a premium.

This much is obvious and well-accepted. There is little need for more studies to document this point. But what are urgently needed are analytical perspectives, methods of analysis, and points of reference in understanding the capacity of firm-specific and region-specific competitive responses to these forces. We argue in subsequent chapters that too much of the literature is transfixed by the continuity of local traditions and institutions while other sections of the academic and policy-related literature on competitiveness and regional economic development are dominated by simple-minded assumptions of flexibility and response. What is needed is a mode of analysis that is sensitive to agents' cognitive capacities, linking those capacities to local circumstances and inherited resources. This is at the core of this particular book. It provides a worked-through argument about the interaction between agents, their environments, and history and geography in the global content.

We have termed our perspective 'agent-centred' in contrast to those perspectives that are institution-centred and those that are market-centred. There is some irony in our agent-centred claims and analytical logic. One of us has been, more often than not, associated with institution-centred arguments in favour of the significance of local circumstances in structuring the options and patterns of competitive response to global integration. The related literature is rich in associated concepts liked 'embeddedness', 'path dependence' and 'sunk costs'. Here we do not so much dispute the significance of these notions as re-order their priority in relation to the cognitive and decision-making capacities of economic agents. For almost a decade, those in favour of 'embeddedness' have fought against the simplicity of neoclassical convergence theorists. In doing so, much has been learnt about the importance of the context and environment in which agents live and work.

At its core, however, we believe that those who argue in favour of the embeddedness of competitive strategy have gone too far; the virtues of this argument in relation to the flexibility school have been such that the strategic responsiveness of economic agents has been less studied. At the same time, those that advance the cause of neoclassical convergence and flexibility models have ignored the cognitive and decision-making capacities of agents; market imperatives dominate, providing an easy way of avoiding focus on economic agents. We do not intend to idealise agents, and we do not suggest that agents are universal entities shorn of social, cultural and community identities. The project, as is seen below, is all about their strategic interaction with context and environment (code words representing local institutions and traditions). We are firmly of the view, however, that too many analysts presume economic agents to be prisoners of the past or the market.

At this point, we should mention that our analytical treatment of these issues has been inspired by the work of Herbert Simon, the Carnegie school of behavioral economics, and recent developments in cognitive science. As such the chapters in this book re-work their insights, drawing connections between related theoretical arguments and recent economic conditions, and driving home implications for the place of economic agents in complex multi-jurisdictional settings. Much of economics, geography and economic geography (in its various disciplinary guises) have yet to come to grips with the insights of the Carnegie School, and analysts are less aware than they should be of the significance or otherwise of assumptions made about agents' cognitive and decision-making capacities. Surely the growth and development of the information and knowledge economy is all about agents' cognition and learning? If innovation and invention are to be the corner stones of European and American growth over the coming century, we need to take these issues far more seriously than hitherto.

Finally, we should be clear at the outset about our argumentative style: while based upon detailed case studies of firms, industries and regions, the book is an exercise in abstraction. We hope to convince the audience that our 'framework' is significant and useful by successive moves of argument rather than evidence. In doing so, we hope that the reader will be inspired to apply the framework to their own circumstances. In that case, we will have been successful in looking forward to a reinvigorated theory of global and regional competitiveness.

Acknowledgements

Support for the project that was the basis of the book was provided by the European Commission through a 5th Framework Grant administered by DG Research over the period 1999–2002. We would like to thank Dr. Marshall Hsia and later Dr. Nikos Kastrinos (the supervisors of our project) for their continued enthusiasm for the project which has become the book. Also important in this respect has been collaboration with our project partners, especially Dr. Helen Lawton Smith (UK), Professor Theo Palaskas and Dr. Maria Tsampra (Greece), Professor Paolo Guerrieri and Dr. Simona Iammarino (Italy), Professor Mary O'Sullivan and Manuela Giangrande (France and Ireland), and Professor Pere Escorsa (Spain). We are pleased to report that the project was productive and intellectually engaging.

Our scientific board, which included Professors Meric Gertler, Colin Mayer, and Ronald Martin, were very helpful in the initial phases of the project and provided timely advice on the project final report and this book manuscript. Each has his own expertise and interests, and each has helped as intellectual points of reference in the evolution of our thinking. None of the above should be held responsible for any opinions or arguments expressed herein.

Throughout the project, we have benefited from the assistance of many people at the University of Oxford. Most significantly, Jan Burke and Madeline Mitchell both managed the electronic network, the exchange of material, and the logistics of the project in ways that have sustained our collaboration and cooperation. Likewise, Jennie McKenzie and Chris White provided crucial administrative and financial support for the project. As for research assistance Jane Battersby, Chlöe Flutter and Merridy Wilson added a great deal of insight and intelligence to the project bringing the data, the literature, and the final report to conclusion. We are very grateful for their enthusiasm, hard work and commitment.

Also important has been the hospitality of the Rothermere American Institute of the University of Oxford. The Institute provided an excellent environment and timely resources for our project. In this regard, we wish to record our warm appreciation for the help provided by Andrea Beighton and Gillian Fullilove.

Various chapters of this book were presented at conferences sponsored by the Association of American Geographers, the Regional Studies Association, and the British Association of American Studies. These events were very useful indeed in clarifying our goals and arguments. Finally, we should also acknowledge the following publishers for permission to republish revised versions of papers that first appeared in scholarly journals. Specifically, Franz Steiner Verlag Wiesbaden GmbH for Gordon L. Clark, Paul Tracey and Helen Lawton Smith 'Agents, endowments and path dependence' in *Geographische Zeitschrift* (2001) 89: 165–180; Blackwell Publishers for Gordon L. Clark, Paul Tracey and Helen Lawton Smith 'Rethinking comparative studies: an agent-centred perspective' in *Global Networks* (2002) 2: 263–284; Blackwell Publishers for Paul Tracey and Gordon L. Clark 'Alliances, networks and competitive strategy: rethinking clusters of innovation' in *Growth and Change* (2003) 34: 1–16; and Taylor and Francis for Paul Tracey, Gordon L. Clark and Helen Lawton Smith 'Cognition, learning and European regional growth: an agent-centred perspective on the 'new' economy' in *Economics of Innovation and New Technology* (2004) 13: 1–18.

Gordon L. Clark and Paul Tracey

1
Introduction

Looking forward over the 21st century, we see the forces of globalisation driving the integration of national and regional economies. In
the developed world, at least, it seems likely that globalisation will
challenge inherited traditions, institutions, and ways of thinking
about the organisation of economy and society. Looking forward,
we see industries being brought to the global marketplace, the
inherited configuration of productive assets increasingly put in play
by the forces of global competition. And looking forward over the
next 25 years, who would disagree that three of the most important
economic and political issues facing nation-states will be: 'How
should "local" firms respond to the forces of globalisation?', 'What
are the advantages and disadvantages of inherited assets for global
competitiveness?' And, 'Where should firms locate to take advantage of the emerging global economy?' There are clearly other
important issues to be addressed. At this point, we simply wish to
emphasise the fact that answers to these questions will have profound consequences for people's long-term employment and
incomes.

Looking back over the 20th century we see a moment in history
wherein the forces of market competition and global integration
were tempered and deflected by war and ideology. In retrospect it
seems that much of the 20th century was about reining in and regulating market competition within the closed walls of nation states
and their allies. Indeed, seen over the long stretch of economic
history, the post World War II settlement and the economic architecture of the Bretton Woods agreement extended for a time the

1

strong role of nation states. Over the last two decades of the 20th century, however, we saw the re-emergence of the forces of cross-border and international economic integration that dominated development for much of the 18th and 19th centuries. Markets have re-emerged from the 20th century to rival nation states as the focus of decision-making, though the balance of power between market globalisation and the status of the nation state remains to be resolved.

Having been engaged in academic research devoted to the dimensions of corporate and firm based competitive strategies in Asia, Europe, and North America it seems obvious that the forces of economic and geographical integration have profoundly affected where firms invest, what technologies they adopt or do not adopt, who they employ and where, how and what they pay their employees (if they still have direct or immediate employees). Our own research, for example, on the competitive strategies of small and medium enterprises in Europe suggests that their competitors may come from as close as the next village or town and as far away as India and China (Tracey, Clark and Lawton-Smith 2001). Likewise, our research in Asia suggests that there are always more competitors eager to come to the global market (Clark and Kim 1995).

It is clear that the gathering forces of globalisation and economic integration pose significant challenges to contemporary academic inquiry and policy-making. There remain many unresolved debates about issues such as the definition of competitiveness, the proper scale of analysis (global, national, regional or firm), the crucial variables (macroeconomic as opposed to microeconomic), and the role and status of industry competition as opposed to local, national and international public policy. One consequence of the re-emerging global economy is a realisation that intellectual innovation is needed; while it may still be true that macroeconomic policy levers like interest rates and government spending can set the parameters for short term national economic performance, it is more than likely that the growth potential of firms is set by their global and regional links, their rate of technological adjustment to international competition, and their capacity to adapt processes and products to rapidly changing market tastes and preferences. Indeed, whereas conventional macroeconomic policy takes as given the borders of the national economy, firms increasingly seek to expand their market reach beyond those borders just as they face new competitors from other nations and places.

In this book, our goal is to help chart ways forward. Our approach is therefore largely analytical rather than empirical. No path-breaking empirical results based upon detailed case-studies and econometrics are reported herein. Rather, we hope our argument is actually an intellectual framework for research on the competitive consequences and dimensions of economic globalisation. Tackled here are the core topics in studies of globalisation: how to study, in a comparative manner, the global region connection; the proper status attributed to economic agents; the role of history and geography in affecting agents' competitive strategies; the interaction between agents and their environments; their cognitive and decision-making capacities; and the transformation of modern economies from production systems to systems of learning with high levels of social and intellectual capital. These topics are summarised at the end of this chapter.

By the end of the book, we hope to convey to the reader why we believe that economic agents are more than passive entities whose imagination is encumbered by the past, and who self-consciously seek ways of going beyond the past to the future. This is one way of coming to terms with the role and significance of history and geography in global and regional competitiveness.

Competitiveness and regional economic performance

Competitiveness continues to be a controversial issue in social science, and particularly in economics. This is partly because the term is often used uncritically and inappropriately in the public domain. It is also, as Reinert (1995) argues convincingly, because the assumptions contained within it contradict many of the tenets of neoclassical economics: 'In a world inhabited by "representative firms" operating under perfect information and with no scale effects ... the term competitiveness is meaningless' (p. 26–27). Perhaps this is why Reich (1990) believed the concept to be more or less meaningless, and Porter (1990) suggested that the term competitiveness is essentially a proxy for productivity. Like Reinert, we consider competitiveness and productivity to be separate issues: although high productivity and efficiency are normally prerequisites for competitiveness, these factors alone do not necessarily result in financial returns or added value. There are many firms (and nations) throughout the world which are efficient but not profitable, and whose employees (and inhabitants) are desperately poor.[1] This is the essence of competitiveness – it refers to the capacity of firms, industries, regions and countries to grow and make profits in markets subjected to international competition, and for this to be translated into sustained higher living standards and domestic income (Scott and Lodge 1985, Maskell et al. 1998, Reinert 1995).

At this point, we do not wish to exaggerate or idealise the prospects and scope of firm-based strategic decision-making. If markets are highly competitive it might reasonably be argued that firms' strategic options are very limited; strategic choice and decision-making in this context may be simply an issue of internal flexibility and adjustment potential in accordance with market signals (Clark 1994). By focusing upon the firm and its strategic choices and decision-making, we do not mean to ignore the context in which such issues are considered and resolved. In point of fact, we argue throughout the book, as many others would also argue, that the time and place of strategic decision-making can have significant implications for those options considered as relevant, those ignored, and those ultimately taken. But whatever the regional bases for decision-making, market scope and prospects have broadened enormously over the past 25 years, working-up the spatial scale from local to regional and national, and now to Europe and the world beyond. Indeed, just as 'local' firms have had opportunities to expand into markets that have taken them away from their local communities, so too have other firms located in faraway jurisdictions come to understand that the commodity and consumer markets of the developed and developing worlds are increasingly open to rival producers whatever their original location of production (Clark et al. 2000a).

There clearly remain, however, considerable tensions between where firms produce and the ultimate market destinations of their products. If, at some point in time in the past, the geographical scale of production matched the geographical scale of final markets, it might have been the case that there was a symbiotic relationship between the organisation of the production process and the configuration of consumer markets. At times, the literature on economic development and growth assumes that this was once the case and goes on to show that the increasing spatial disjunction between the site of production and the geographical scope of markets has increased the premium placed upon the strategic capacity of those firms that still have a distinctive and committed place of origin. Much of the literature focuses upon the mobility of capital in relation to the configuration of final demand; in Europe at least, given that in many industries small and medium enterprises are the dominant unit of production, we should be less sanguine about the prospects of firms relocating in relation to the imperatives of market competition. In many cases, relocation is less the option than designing and implementing changes to the organisation of production and the technology of production itself.

It must be recognised, however, that conventional models of regional economic growth begin with rather different assumptions. Being dominated by Anglo-American theoretical presumptions and a distinctive heritage of empirical research, much of the literature assumes high levels of factor mobility, and ultimately spatial and economic convergence, measured by employment and welfare (Barro and Sala-I-Martin 1995). By implication, also assumed is at least a national market for firms in an industry and relatively low transaction costs, both with respect to the distance to market and the flow of commodities between firms within related chains of transactions that produce the products and services brought to market. Clearly, the case in point is the US economy and, by extension, NAFTA. Just as obviously, those that advocate a single integrated European market have in mind an institutional configuration that would at least mimic the US case, particularly in terms of enhancing the efficient allocation of capital and labour between the regions of Europe. If European firms are 'embedded' in their local jurisdictions, in the end it is hoped that European market integration may transform existing geographical constraints into an extensive geographical opportunity set.[2]

These theoretical and empirical expectations have been challenged in recent years by the new economic geography allied with Paul Krugman (1991) but shared with many economic geographers whatever their disciplinary heritage (see Clark et al. 2000b). If we introduce increasing as opposed to constant returns to scale then it is possible that individual firms may wish to concentrate at one site while developing local networks of intensive linkages that in effect share between firms the benefits of increasing returns to scale. If we also assume that 'learning by doing' characterises many firms' experience in exploiting their inherited productive assets, there may be considerable benefits in sticking with past investments while adopting new forms of technology that reinforce their knowledge-base (the logic of path dependence). And finally, if we assume that knowledge spills over between firms within an industry by virtue of the movement of labour between related and not so related firms, a firm's labour productivity may develop in accordance with its co-location with other firms. Assuming limited geographical mobility of labour, there is a theoretical rationale for linking-up the competitiveness of firms with the attributes of regions (as suggested by Cooke and Morgan 1998).

At the limit, we can assume firms' competitiveness to be dependent upon their location in region and industry specific regimes of accumulation. And it is possible, at the limit, that those firms' competitive strategies are both enabled and limited by their region-industry setting. To suppose that this is actually the case, however, would be to assume a distinctive theory of agent cognition and decision-making. To make the argument work, we must suppose that entrepreneurs' imagination and capacity for innovation is so tightly structured that their options are *derived* from their contexts rather than developed either through interaction or complete independence from those contexts. As we show elsewhere in this book, this is an unlikely theory of cognition and decision-making (see Chapters 3, 4 and 5). Here, then, is our point of departure for the book: it has to do with how we should conceptualise decision-making and innovation given the fact that all economic agents begin from a point in time and space and compete with one-another over regions, nations and the global economy.

Agent decision-making in time and space

For many years, the study of decision-making was a relatively small field of endeavour in the social sciences. For all the newfound significance attributed to the work by Herbert Simon (1986, 1997) (Nobel laureate in economics) and his colleagues, those genuinely concerned with understanding the scope and nature of human decision-making were consigned to the margins of disciplinary respectability. And yet, over the past decade, there has been remarkable growth in research about decision-making from a wide variety of social science perspectives. Characteristically, this research is driven by a commitment to better understand empirically how and why people make the decisions they do. Even so, why has decision-making been so marginal to the social sciences? In economics and finance, for example, the answer is surely obvious: the theoretical building blocks of the nascent science relied upon an ordered and tractable analytical logic that enabled the generalisation and summing-up of individual behaviour across economies and societies. Textbooks are dominated by this analytical imperative: at base, the rational utility maximising model holds sway over the vast territory of social science affecting the study of all kinds of economic activity including labour productivity, industrial organisation, and economic development.

In essence, the study of decision-making has been dominated by a golden-rule. By definition, all people act according to their best interests and, in doing so, are rational in the sense that they choose the best or optimal course of action most consistent with their goals. This means that people are assumed to systematically assess all possible options for action in accordance with their acknowledged interests. To think otherwise, to suppose that people are neither so systematic (re options for action) nor as focused upon their ultimate interests (re their goals), is to suppose that they are irrational or at least inconsistent. At this point in the argument, Charles Darwin comes to the rescue of the theorist of rationality in the form of an assumption about market efficiency: surely failures of rationality and consistency are stripped out of the market by virtue of the acquisitive instincts of those who are more rational and more consistent than their competitors. This is less a theory of decision-making than it is a normative theory of how the whole system should function given assumptions about deeply-seated competitive instincts.

Of course, it has been widely recognised for many years that non-rational behaviour and decision-making is more common than assumed. Whole disciplines like anthropology and cultural studies have developed in opposition to the perceived narrowness and isolation of the golden-rule from many aspects of social life. Surely social identity and social commitment make a difference to decision-making. Surely these attributes of social life provide important parameters for setting the options for action as well as the ultimate goals of many people. These ideas have been applied to understanding observed behaviour and decision-making (in general) and financial decision-making (in particular). But for all the observation of actual behaviour and decision-making in relation to culture and society, this research has had less impact than we might have expected. In part, this is because 'culture' has been invoked as a counter golden-rule: by this logic, it is tempting to reduce behaviour and decision-making to cultural imperatives (which differ from culture to culture). Also important has been a subtle rank ordering of behaviour and decision-making allowing for the co-existence of all kinds of behaviour: from the ephemeral (presumably dominated by culture) to the market-related (presumably dominated by rationality).

By rational decisions we mean decision-making amongst choices and consequent action, based upon either deductive logic or inductive logic. This much is clear. But when performed by people, rational decision-making seems always less than optimal. People are not ideally rational: reasoning by means of propositions and quantified experiences is notoriously poor. Syllogistic reasoning is impaired by the 'atmosphere effect': people tend to accept erroneously an affirmative conclusion to do something if the premises are affirmative. Furthermore, arguments involving sequences of sentences with multiple quantifiers appear to be beyond people's computational capacities (Clark and Marshall 2002). It has been argued (somewhat controversially) that many of our reasoning heuristics evolved in the Pliocene, an era in which they were well suited to the social and physical environment of our hunter-gatherer ancestors. Now that the environment has changed beyond recognition, some of these 'innate' strategies may still be useful but others have become maladaptive (see Gigerenzer and Todd 1999 on 'fast and frugal heuristics'). In response, anchoring tasks in concrete settings is essential for reasoning even if oftentimes misleading.

To make a rational decision in the real world is to choose as best as possible between a set of alternatives. The phrase 'as best as possible' is intended to contrast with 'optimally', emphasising the physical and psychological constraints that may render it humanly impossible for the decision-maker to follow ideal-rationality to perfection. Such decisions clearly involve: the acquisition of information relevant to choice; the appraisal of the values attached to the possible outcomes of different choices; and the assessment of the probability of occurrence of each of those possible outcomes. The final decision will then be made on the basis of some combination of these three factors. Normative approaches have typically emphasised the latter two factors, no doubt because they can in principle be quantified and subjected to mathematical analysis. In markets, however, all three elements are significant. But it is unlikely that the resultant ideal-rational construct – economic man – will behave in the same way as psychological man or woman. While we may idealise decision-making, invoking theories derived from economics and finance, we remain biological entities subject to systematic constraints on cognitive capacity.

Even so, we do observe ourselves and others' behaviour. We can learn. And we can adjust how we behave by making decisions by conscious effort.[3] Indeed, our ability to reflect upon our actions, intentions, and motives mark us profoundly different from other biological entities. In this sense, we should not be overly pessimistic about observed errors of judgement, mistakes of recognition, and prejudices that seem to characterise so much of our decision-making. Left to our own devices we are risk adverse, overly sensitive to the short-run, and too often affected by immediate events rather than the discernable patterns of events over time and space. But many of us have mechanisms for monitoring our actions and also mechanisms that alert us to known shortcomings. This is also one important function of institutions – to be centres of competence that transcend the idiosyncrasies of individual decision-making. Likewise, this is one role of expert advisors – to go beyond 'local' situations, prompting reflection and encouraging better decisions. While it would be foolish to pretend that institutions are necessarily more efficient than individuals, the organisation of knowledge and the institutional processing of information are important industries in their own right.

Individuals are also distinguished by an ability to collaborate with others. For some theorists this is a defining characteristic, the one that underpins our capacity to create opportunities and induce change, and a crucial component of global and regional competitiveness.

Mayntz (1993) argued that the development of networks and alliances has shown itself to be intrinsic to 'societal modernization', and that where individuals and organizations obtain a degree of autonomy from political and religious control they will tend to seek to further their objectives through collaboration with others. She gives the example of the collapse of the former East Germany where the dominant political party exerted pervasive and omnipresent control over virtually all aspects of the country's economy and society, and where even minimal local autonomy was denied. East Germany's demise should not, Mayntz argued, be thought of simply as a violent reaction against decades of political repression, but as the consequence of a system which deliberately and systematically stifled innovation and prevented local flexibility and responsiveness – a position which became increasingly untenable in the context of the growing success and self-confidence of its western neighbour. Conceptually, Mayntz places autonomous agents with the capacity to act responsibly, to make conscious choices, and to form alliances voluntarily and deliberately at the core of sophisticated and 'modern' socio-economic systems. See also Bathelt and Glückler (2003), and Bathelt, Malmberg and Maskell (2002).

And yet such informal collaboration cannot be incorporated within the rational choice paradigm: rational and self-interested actors would not deliberately participate in alliances in the absence of legal or contractual protection, nor would they exhibit the reciprocity required of such relationships. That they do so provides further evidence of the shortcomings of rational choice as a valid framework within which to consider economic activity. But it is also a reminder that informal networks, and behaviour more generally, are positioned within wider institutional structures which impose boundaries to accepted behaviour and generate the conditions for the existence of such networks (Scharpf 1993). Archer (1996) noted that it is common among human beings across time and space to 'feel both free and enchained', a contradiction she described as 'the most pressing social problem of the human condition' (p. xii). In economics and geography, explanations of behaviour continue to be, in Archer's terms, entirely deterministic, entirely objectivistic or exclusively microscopic. Rationalism has given way to institutionalism, with proponents tending to proceed either by collapsing institutional structure and individual behaviour, or by prioritising the former over the latter to such a degree that agents appear almost passive, overpowered by the constraints imposed upon them by institutions. Either way the firm remains, for all intents and purposes, as the proverbial black box.

An important lesson to be drawn from social theorists such as Archer (1996, 2000) and Mouzelis (1995) is that a clear distinction must be drawn between agents and the social structures of the places they inhabit if either are to be useful and coherent analytical concepts (Healy 1998). This is what we have tried to do in this book. We discuss in some depth the central role that social institutions play in global and regional competitiveness and we emphasise the very real contribution that scholars working in the institutional tradition have made to understanding economic behaviour. But, and as is suggested in the title of this book, a large part of our thinking is devoted to agency, partly because it has been so neglected in the study of economic activity, and partly because it goes to the heart of our subject matter. Our view is that there is a cognitive dimension both to knowledge (in the sense that information requires a cognitive framework for it to become knowledge), and to institutions (in the sense that agents rely on institutions for developing their cognitive frameworks and for interpreting the world around them). See Nooteboom (2000, 2001 and 2002).

Looking forward

With these arguments as points of reference, the book proceeds in the following manner. To launch the theoretical argument of the whole book, in Chapter 2 we begin by observing that there have been many projects comparing and contrasting social and economic phenomena across the regions of Europe. Broadly speaking, three rival approaches to comparative research can be identified. One suggests that the study of different countries and their regions is unproblematic. Stress is placed on an integrated theoretical perspective emphasising apparent similarities while explaining differences by reference to the heritage of nations and places. By way of contrast, a second approach relies on case studies and presumes the existence of profound differences between countries and regions. Stress is placed upon the local cultural, social and political factors that sustain persistent difference. A third approach argues for the significance of national institutional frameworks, supposing that those frameworks limit and structure agents' decisions and actions. Whatever their differences, idealism drives each method of comparative study. We consider these rival theories of comparative study, and suggest an alternative model based upon a set of fundamental assumptions about the nature of human cognition. These assumptions are the building blocks for our analysis (as noted above). We focus in particular upon consciousness and reflexivity, the interplay between agency and structure, and the connection between intention and rationality. Implications are then drawn for study of competitiveness and comparative studies. In the penultimate section of the chapter we comment on the limits of comparative studies emphasising the problems that lie behind the translation of complex concepts within and between languages.

From this reference point, in Chapter 3 we emphasise the links between agent-centred decision-making and the role and status of the context in which decision-making takes place. Our problem is simple yet complex: how can we explain the acknowledged importance of path dependence while allowing for agents to step away (even defect) from local imperatives in the light of European integration and globalisation? To answer this question requires adding on three conceptual building blocks to our previously introduced framework. Beginning with a critique of W.B. Arthur's notion of path dependency and drawing upon the work of Herbert Simon, we introduce a *contingent* model of rationality and decision-making. We then suggest how and why social customs and norms – relational capital – may be important place-specific *endowments* at worst constraining, perhaps neutralising, sometimes enabling, and at best promoting agents' decision-making. Given a *multi-jurisdictional environment*, the third piece of the analysis concentrates on the process whereby agents may take advantage of the possibilities offered by other jurisdictions (a common-scale process of competition and differentiation). Implications are drawn for the role and importance of place-specific relational capital in the context of accelerating global competition. While recognising the empirical reality of path-dependence, we dispute the necessity of its persistence.

Following this crucial intervention, in Chapter 4 we begin by challenging deterministic approaches to decision-making that assume action can be reduced to structural constraints, arguing that the environment in which firms operate is dynamic rather than static, and that firms have a demonstrated capacity for strategic choice. In doing so, this chapter extends the previously introduced framework regarding the role and significance of agents in economic and geographical integration. Following on from this, we consider networks of interaction, which have assumed particular significance in recent years because of their presumed importance for learning and innovation. Alliances between related firms are thought to encourage interactive learning between participating organisations through the sharing of knowledge and information, which is itself facilitated through trust, shared values and ways of working. The vast body of literature that has emerged is, however, incredibly fragmented, encompassing an array of theoretical positions and perspectives. We focus upon two issues which we believe to be of particular significance and which need clarification in order to move to a clearer understanding of the ways in which networks of interaction evolve, and of their capabilities and limitations in relation to economic performance and competitiveness: (1) the importance of network structure, arguing that innovative activity requires flexibility with regard to network formation; (2) the role of geography in relation to the construction and functioning of alliances. It is our contention that networks are likely to be increasingly international in scope.

In the penultimate chapter of the book, we extend our framework to the new economy comparing the US and Europe. Quintessentially a US phenomenon, the information and knowledge economy combines regional clusters of innovation with new and sophisticated forms of intellectual and finance capital. Regions such as Silicon Valley in California and Route 128/495 Boston have excelled in technologically sophisticated, knowledge-based industries such as telecommunications, information technology and software development. They have won praise for their innovativeness, entrepreneurship and phenomenal growth, and have been central to the remarkable renaissance of the US economy over the last two decades. Although some point to similar regions in Europe, there is widespread concern that Europe cannot match the innovativeness of the US. For those European economies struggling to adjust to global competition, the information and knowledge economy is seen as the panacea. It is regarded as a proven recipe for all places and sectors, with the potential to remedy structural weaknesses that have become ever more apparent in a world subject to globalisation, increased international competition, and technological change.

This chapter begins with the information and knowledge economy as a source of wealth creation and competitive advantage. Building on previous chapters, we use our agent-centred perspective to consider the information and knowledge economy, stressing the significance of cognition and learning for innovation while making the connection between organisations and their environments. It is argued that the information and knowledge economy is complex and multi-faceted, and cannot be transposed easily between cultures: it is underpinned by place-specific features of social and spatial organisation which act as resources for actors and promote collective action. We conclude the chapter by drawing together the implications of our approach for European economic development.

In Chapter 7 we bring the book to a close, noting the avenues for future research opened-up by our arguments.

Coda

We should pause, for a moment, before going on to the substantive chapters of the book to consider a possible objection to our project. The objection we foresee can be stated as follows: by focusing upon the cognitive and decision-making capacities of economic agents we, in effect, idealise individuals both in terms of their relevance to the study of economic geography and in terms of their status in relation to social and political structure. Taking this point further, some critics may argue that we privilege individuals as if social structure and the distribution of political power are secondary to their theoretical role as the driving force behind economic matters. Furthermore, it could be said that we effectively strip economic agents of their social identity, thereby rendering any discussion of their place in civil society as superfluous or irrelevant. At worst, our analytical logic may be thought destructive of valuable local traditions, loyalties and commitments. In any event, it could be argued that we attribute too much significance to decision-making given the over-whelming forces of globalisation and economic integration.[4]

We find it difficult to accept the charge that by focusing upon the cognitive and decision-making capacities of economic agents we ignore or trivialise history and geography. Throughout the book, our point of reference is precisely the interaction between economic agents' decision-making and the contexts in which they live, work, and may wish to escape. We are very conscious of the need to situate economic agents in space and time believing that to do otherwise is to build empty castles in the sky. Clearly, economic agents must take into account and do take into account the fact that they live in certain places and have a set of opportunities and capacities that are the product of social, economic and political developments over long stretches of time. But having acknowledged the significance of history and geography does not mean that *ipso facto* economic agents must somehow drop out of the analytical equation. Our book is all about the role and competitive significance of history and geography from the vantage point of economic agents.[5]

Most importantly, our project was deliberately conceived to challenge those who believe that history and geography are of such profound significance that economic agents are solely creatures of the past. There are two reasons for this point of departure. In the first instance, we are convinced that history and geography should not be read in such a determinant manner and that social identity itself is far more open to debate and dissent than is often assumed. We could, at this point, invoke all kinds of post-modern commentary on the multiplicity of identity and the social construction of identities given a world where culture and consumption are far more significant than we would otherwise recognise (see, for example, Thrift 2000). Surely the deep debate occasioned by the emerging fiscal crisis of European states is testament enough to the deep divisions in many societies about what society is and what individuals are in relation to social commitments and obligations (Clark 2001).

European integration is, in part, a project about providing economic agents from various regions with a scaled-up regulatory framework in which they are able to accumulate more effectively economic resources and make decisions about the best use of those resources across the economic landscape. Surely the goal of European integration, according to the single market ethos, is a goal informed by a commitment to economic agents as the building block of long-term wealth and income. Granted it is hardly ever officially discussed in this manner. But it seems to us a most important argument about the relative significance of history and geography in relation to a united Europe. Perhaps it is precisely this issue which informs right-wing hostility to the European project. In that case, we would place ourselves firmly with those who see the long-term advantages of European integration just as we would ally ourselves with the forces of progressive social and political development in Europe for people of all kinds and nationalities.

2
Agents and Institutions

Comparative study has always played a prominent role in evaluating theories of economic resource allocation (witness the literature on regional economic convergence and divergence; see Clark et al. 1986 and Martin 2001). More recently, however, economic analysis throughout the world has come to rely upon cross-national comparisons of local and regional systems of accumulation, innovation and production (witness the literature on the Third Italy, Baden Württemberg, Silicon Valley etc; see Storper and Salais 1997). Reference to other countries and regions, comparing and contrasting competitiveness and economic trajectories, has encouraged analysts to look beyond conventional explanations of regional differentiation to issues such as culture, social capital, and the formal and informal regulation of exchange relationships (see Thrift 2000).

Most obviously, concern about the forces driving globalisation and its impact on nations, regions, and localities has brought into the open an urgent need for comparative studies. How else are we to assess the significance of globalisation in relation to the forces of local differentiation? Indeed, it could be argued that debate over globalisation is essentially a debate about comparison and contrast (Crouch and Streeck 1997). In this regard, new connections are being made between those who research competition between whole systems of economic governance (see, for example, Dore 2000), and those who analyse the place of regions in relation to national and international economic trends (see, for example, Clark et al. 2000a). At the same time, of course, governments and various

multilateral institutions have become strong advocates for comparative studies providing the funding base for large-scale cross-country
comparative analyses of competitiveness and economic integration.

There are a variety of methods of comparative study justified by
claims and counter-claims. These are often rival approaches rather
than complementary or supplementary methods. Our goal in this
chapter is to identify and explain the basic assumptions behind
three particular methods of comparative study before setting out our
own agenda. Contrasts are drawn between ideal types and the commonalities between empirical methods ignored for the purposes of
clarity. While our focus is reserved for comparative economic and
geographical research, our arguments apply across the social sciences and are relevant to the study of all kinds of places. Perhaps
most obviously, our approach is suited to the study of national
systems of regulation devoted to innovation, labour markets and
finance. We also consider it to have relevance to a much broader
range of issues such as, for example, the growing bodies of work on
global cities, citizenship and welfare systems. We cannot hope to
cover every segment of literature appropriate to our argument. By
virtue of our rather different backgrounds, we refer to the relevant
literatures in economics, geography and management studies. It is
important to note, moreover, that we promote a distinctive perspective on agents and institutions. To summarise, we align our argument with the Carnegie School of behaviour and economics (see
Simon 1986). This implies particular assumptions about the nature
of human cognition and rationality not always shared across the
disciplines (compare Jensen 1998).

In the next section, we present three models of comparative study
which have their roots in three different branches of social science.
Our intention is both to assess common approaches to comparative
research as well as their inter-relationships. This leads to our own
approach, an argument about the relationship between agents and
institutions, and an assessment of the limits of comparative study.
As is well appreciated, in comparative studies there are significant
conflicts over interpretation and meaning that may, in part, be
attributed to differences of language and culture. In our case, we
attribute much of such conflict to the complex nature of many
social scientific concepts. We discuss this issue in more detail in the
penultimate section of the chapter.

Models of comparative studies

A premium has been placed upon understanding the differences between countries and regions throughout the world, and the prospects for harmonisation and/or convergence to international best practice. Whether this is a viable means of analysing globalisation, whether this is representative of the economic power of global corporations, and whether this is a plausible long-term political trend (the re-scaling of administrative and political powers upwards as opposed to the decentralisation of power downwards away from national institutions) are all issues widely debated in the literature. They are also profound questions not easily answered at this point in time (see Swyngedouw 2000 and Wiener 1999). We simply observe that a vibrant market for comparative study has developed over the past few decades, transforming the field from an individual and discipline-centred activity into a more systematic endeavour funded in accordance with the agendas of national and international policy makers and executed through international teams of social science researchers drawn from participating or related nations.[1] This is perhaps most obvious in the European Union, but can be found throughout the developed and developing world (witness the related roles of the UN, the OECD and the World Bank).[2]

One of the most difficult aspects of comparative economic research is finding suitable units of analysis. Many projects begin with an ideal type of firm and/or industry and an idealised region that provides the context for study. However, there are obviously significant differences in the operation and social organisation of capitalist economies throughout the world – differences exist between nominally similar firms, industries and regions, as well as between the institutions that form the basis of economic governance. Crouch and Streeck (1997) argued that capitalist economies vary in at least four ways. (1) Competitive markets and organisational hierarchies differ significantly in terms of their responsibilities and their mode of operation; (2) various levels of involvement of the state in the management of private companies have led to different rules and outcomes; (3) the functioning of markets and firms are often systematically different depending upon co-operation between competitors, rules governing the interaction of firms with competing interests, and the involvement of formal associations such as trade unions in the labour process; (4) informal communities and networks control large proportions of the transactions in many economies. This has helped sustain as well as change systems of governance.

Entwined in arguments about the significance of capitalist diversity, as well as the significance of culture and language more generally, are particular views about the proper model of comparative study. It is all too easy to attribute misapprehension and misunderstanding to others' barely recognised context-specific motives and behaviour. By implication, comparative study is as much a question of ethnography (being itself the object of study) as it is a method of analysis useful in joining together the tapestry of humanity. While there is an important role for understanding comparative studies as a social practice, we would also contend that there are marked disagreements within and between the social sciences about the proper methods of comparative study. There are three rather different methods of comparative research that co-exist and compete with one another for dominance. In this section we look at each method as a model of social science.

Theory-centred models of comparative study, emphasised most obviously in economics, assume that the study of different countries and/or regions is largely unproblematic. Stress is placed upon an integrated theoretical perspective applicable to the world at large. This approach is rooted in an over-arching normative conception of human behaviour as rational or at least predictable. Implied is a belief that we can apply the laws of human behaviour and organisation to different settings just as natural scientists use first principles to explain the natural landscape. The notion of rationality has great appeal when seeking to understand societies and economies; it provides a common method of explanation which simplifies the research process by assuming concepts can be translated easily between cultures and languages. Over much of the twentieth century theoretical axioms based upon the assumption of predictability dominated the social sciences, and remain powerful reference points for any argument to the contrary.[3] In economics, for instance, neo-classical theories based upon the assumption of rational-individual maximising behaviour continue to form the core of the subject (Hodgson 1996). Likewise in sociology, functionalism

and structural-functionalism, threads of theory that together consider the rationalisation of action to be crucial to social practice,
continue as influential reference points albeit less important than
during the 1970s and 1980s (Coleman 1990).

To the extent that theory-centred approaches to comparative
study are concerned with similarity and difference, they tend to be
used to clarify and develop generality. This does not mean that the
design of comparative study is unimportant. Setting the parameters
of study, controlling for the known effects of common factors, and
ensuring the integrity of collected data are vital to evaluating
theory. Derived comparative data are then often analysed using
sophisticated and well-accepted statistical and/or econometric techniques which, in turn, leads to the development of better forms of
empirical estimation and analysis. By this logic, comparative
research is partly concerned with establishing common truths and
general implications. Not surprisingly, it is a mode of inquiry often
favoured by funding agencies and research councils. The alternative
seems, more often than not, to be arbitrary and subjective: studies
which take a less 'scientific' approach are deemed to be either misleading or unhelpful in the drive towards a common understanding
of accepted problems.

By contrast, the *case-centred approach to comparative study*, which
owes much to anthropology, presumes the existence of profound
and persistent differences between countries and regions. As such it
might be thought to be a 'principled' reaction against the idea that
universals exist to be 'discovered' through theory-centred investigation of others (Geertz 1974). In this vein, anthropological and
related research seeks to document diversity while recognising the
problems inherent in conceptualising social life from just one perspective or place. Fundamental to the case-centred approach is the
assumption that the social world is so complex and diverse that it
cannot be fully understood. Geertz (1974, p. 29) suggested 'I...
[have never] gotten anywhere near to the bottom of anything I
have ever written about... Cultural analysis is intrinsically incomplete. And, worse than that, the more deeply it goes the more
incomplete it is'.

By this account, any search for generalisations about human
beings and their actions needs to begin with dialogue with
members of the culture studied, gradually improving understanding

through an interactive recursive process of mutual learning. Here, comparative research is understood as a social practice wherein people are studied *in* their worlds as opposed to being the raw data for universal axioms about *the* world. In the most extreme form, case-centred versions of comparative study are self-defeating. At the limit there is a belief that we cannot ascribe common meaning to the world, and the corollary belief that to examine the world in a comparative sense would be pointless. Dierkes and Wagner (1992, p. 626) were concerned that if this model was to dominate social science, the entire project of comparative study would be discredited. By their account there was a danger that the project would be lost to 'strands of more or less formal or imaginative theorising that increasingly... decouple[s] themselves from any reference to reality... The objective will often be just to add another story about the world to already existing ones. And empirical research, which, all methodological sophistication notwithstanding, will implicitly adhere to a naive empirical realism and will contribute little to the understanding of modern society, will be the quantitatively largest case study'.

There is an obvious alternative to the two approaches outlined above which can be summarised as the *institution-centred approach to comparative study*. In many ways, this approach owes its origins to the so-called new (or neo-) institutional economics. Although there are distinct and competing theoretical positions within new institutionalism, at its core are two basic claims: (1) that capitalism can (or should) be understood by examining differences in the economic, political and social institutional structures of societies (Crouch and Streeck 1997); and (2) that institutions provide the strategic context for agents' decision-making (Steinmo and Tolbert 1998). By this logic, institutions shape the choices faced by individuals and therefore help explain differences between countries as well as the development of policy within them. In some respects, however, the new institutional economics may be less of a departure from mainstream neo-classical economics and rational assumptions of social practice than assumed (North 1990, compare with Hodgson 1996). Curiously, assumptions about the rational and optimising behaviour of human agents are embedded in the new institutionalism even if individuals, their behaviour, their goals and their beliefs are more or less taken for granted.

In this model, institutions are considered to be the most important influence on individual behaviour, forming the boundaries of individuals' options and choices. The possibility that the behaviour, aims and aspirations of individuals might be influenced by social factors other than institutions is not considered unless 'institution' is a code word for social processes, codes and practices of all kinds. In some instances, institutions are thought to profoundly affect individuals' sense of themselves (especially referencing cultural attributes), whereas in other instances institutions are assumed to provide a framework for individual action Further, the possibility that there might be conflict between individuals and institutions is often glossed over, as are the mechanisms whereby individuals are shaped by social cultures that change over time.[4] It is difficult to be entirely definitive about the institutional approach; it subsumes many competing ideas under a rather simple umbrella. Nevertheless, the connection between new institutional economics and traditional neo-classical approaches to social science has led some scholars to question detailed accounts of the role of institutions in the development of societies. Such accounts may merely be *post-hoc* revisionist explanations for societal differences that have common or uncommon causes.

All three approaches to comparative study can be disputed. At best, they provide a partial recipe for research, and the ideas and assumptions disregarded by each often form the basis of competing methods of comparative study. Furthermore, research questions often tend towards particular models, which may form the most suitable approach in particular circumstances. For example, the theory-centred approach is surely most appropriate for testing generality. It would be a mistake to imagine that the case-centred approach is better suited to this purpose: in many respects the objective of research in this instance presupposes the kind of model to be used. It is also true, of course, that research objectives are themselves strongly influenced by the epistemological and ontological positions adopted by researchers. It would be unusual for scholars who held the view that reality is a social construction to engage in the testing of theory. Thus we would argue that while the three approaches outlined above can be thought of as rivals in competition with one another, in many instances research questions have their own methodological domain around which specific interests are moulded.

If we were to sample contemporary comparative social science literature we would find it split between the first (theory-centred) and third (institution-centred) approaches. If we were to look back over the past 25 years, the first approach would dominate the third. More recently, however, the institution-centred approach has gained popularity as the focus of comparative economic and geographical research has shifted from gross generalisations of competing economic systems to the assessment of the diversity within market based systems of accumulation (Storper 1995). Furthermore, with the shift of focus towards regional systems of accumulation within the context of an increasingly globalised world accounting for differences in observed outcomes (holding industry and firm size constant), much comparative research has come to rely upon institutional (local and national) differences to drive explanation.

Agent-centred comparative study

For sceptics of the theory-centred approach to comparative studies, social science runs the risk of being little more than the determination of 'logical conclusions from pre-ordained assumptions... attempts to address the real world, or to evaluate basic assumptions on the basis of evidence, are downgraded' (Hodgson 1996, p. 2176). Following Sayer (1992, p. 189), we believe that the notion of self-contained, rational and optimising agents formed apart from the social world is a 'contentless abstraction'. By contrast, we begin with the assumption that agents' actions and interests are formed within particular societies characterised by formal and informal customs and norms that sustain behaviour. Leading on from these propositions we can make at least three other criticisms of the theory-centred approach to comparative studies: (1) it is unable to deal with and take account of social conflict. For the most part, societies and economies are naively answered homogenous with individuals sharing core values, beliefs and norms; (2) it presumes a static view of culture, and has difficulty in explaining how and why societies may change over time if the forces driving change are not obviously economic; (3) and perhaps most importantly, it is unable to account fully for agents' ascription of meaning to the world.

We are also sympathetic to the case-centred approach. It makes impossible demands on our imagination. In order to understand social phenomena in different countries it seems we must focus on the accounts of social actors in their 'local' contexts. While we understand the difficulties inherent in translating concepts from one culture to another, we find it hard to accept the implication that those engaged in comparative research cannot question or interpret the narratives of social actors from different cultures. In general terms, such narratives cannot provide complete accounts of historical and structural complexity. We would also argue that individuals external to societies may be able to conceptualise local circumstances in informative and useful ways. For some critics, the case-centred approach to comparative study cannot deal with the causal factors that create and perpetuate the structural and institutional aspects of societies and economies. Rex (1974, p. 50) argued that social scientists are better able to understand 'actual historical structures... and not merely the structures which actors believe to exist, or believe that they make, in the process of thinking them to exist'. In other words, the social constructions of situated agents form only one part of a wider world in which they live.

We are not entirely critical of institutional approaches to comparative research. So much of public policy, whatever the nature of society, properly assumes that institutions regulate and promote certain kinds of behaviour while disallowing or penalising other kinds of behaviour.[5] And like many approaches to social science, the institution-centred approach assumes that agents behave in ways related to institutional incentives. Still it may be subject to some of the criticisms of the theory-centred approach (an inability to take account of social conflict and cultural change and an inability to deal with the ascription of meaning). Although institutions are fundamental to the ways in which societies and economies develop and are therefore crucial to comparative enquiry, we do not conceive agents as being essentially passive and inert, located within an institutional framework in which their cognition is either dominated or perpetually constrained. In this sense, too much is made of institutional structure. Surely the advent of globalisation has brought into question the coherence and persistence of local institutions and the nation state? While we believe that institutions enable and facilitate decisions and actions, we do not accept their claimed pre-eminent status in social theory or in contemporary life.

In view of the limitations inherent in the models outlined above, it is important to rethink comparative research (see Table 2.1 summarising the three competing approaches and our alternative). One way to proceed is to invoke what some theorists term as an agent-centred approach. To illustrate this approach, assume the firm is the unit of analysis. In market-based economies decisions about prices, levels of production, products and the use of resources are made by agents in a range of institutions in the public and private sectors. Many of these decisions are made within firms, themselves complex organisations (Cyert and March 1992). In addition to the capacity to make routine and sequential decisions, agents have the capacity to learn, even if this varies between types of organisation (Cyert and March 1992, Senge 1992). They have a demonstrated ability to detect and correct weaknesses in their operating procedures by scanning the environment, setting goals and objectives, and reviewing performance in relation to these goals (single-loop learning). Information systems are often developed for this purpose. The ability to question the relevance of more fundamental aspects of the operation of institutions (double-loop learning) may be far more difficult, particularly for firms that are structured in highly bureaucratic ways. This would involve the questioning of deep-rooted assumptions, which may be deliberately set aside in relation to more immediate functional objectives (Morgan 1997).

Despite these obvious capacities, we do not consider agents or firms to be so rational that they are always and everywhere utility maximisers (compare Jensen 1998). As Morgan (1997) points out, firms may pursue goals and encourage their members to conceive of decision-making as a rational and efficient process, but organisations contain many kinds of rationality. They are at the same time systems of cooperation and competition: employees are required to work together in order to achieve stated aims and objectives, but may also be competing with one another for resources and power. In other words, rationality is 'always interest-based and thus changes according to the perspective from which it is viewed' (Morgan 1997, p. 209). In the remainder of this section we outline our own agent-centred approach to comparative enquiry which focuses primarily on the nature of human cognition, while acknowledging informational and institutional constraints. The agent-centred model contains four basic propositions.

Table 2.1 Typology of four methods comparative studies

	Assumptions	Strengths	Weaknesses
Theory-centred	1. Theoretically, comparative research is largely unproblematic. 2. Human behaviour is essentially rational and predictable. 3. The 'laws' of human behaviour and organisation can be applied universally to different settings. 4. Concerned with establishing common truths and general implications.	1. Renders the process of comparative study relatively straightforward. 2. Often produces unambiguous results which can be supported 'scientifically' using sophisticated statistical/ econometric techniques.	1. Oversimplifies human behaviour and cognition. 2. Unable to take account of social conflict. 3. Presumes a static view of culture and institutional change. 4. Cannot account for agent's ascription of meaning. 5. Can sometimes be little more than the determination of logical conclusions from predetermined assumptions.
Case-centred	1. Comparative research is a very complex and demanding undertaking. Indeed, the social world is so complex that it cannot be fully understood. 2. Profound and persistent differences between countries and regions. 3. Rationality is relative and socially constructed.	1. Allows phenomena to be studied in their 'natural' setting. 2. Provides detailed and deeply textured data based on 'local' accounts. 3. Recognises the existence of different interpretations of common concepts. 4. Treats differing interpretations of common concepts equally (avoids cultural imperialism).	1. Cannot provide a complete account of a society's historical complexity. 2. Cannot explain fully institutional change 3. Exaggerates the difficulties inherent in translating concepts from one culture to another.

Table 2.1 Typology of four methods comparative studies – *Continued*

	Assumptions	Strengths	Weaknesses
	4. The researcher(s) must enter into dialogue with members of the culture being studied, gradually improving understanding through an interactive process of mutual learning.		
Institution-centred	1. Capitalism may be understood by examining differences in the economic, political and social institutional structures of societies. 2. Institutions provide the strategic context for agents' decision making. 3. Institutions are the most important influence on human behaviour, forming the boundaries of individuals' options and choices. 4. Assumes that human behaviour is essentially rational and predictable.	1. Assumes that institutions are fundamental to the ways in which societies and economies develop and therefore crucial to comparative enquiry. 2. Properly assumes that institutions may regulate and promote certain kinds of behaviour while disallowing or penalising other kinds. 3. Assumes that agents behave in ways which are consistent and predictable in relation to institutional incentives.	1. Marginalises the role of agents in the formation of institutions. 2. Tends to idealise the coherence of the institutional structure in which agents operate. 3. Assumes that agents are essentially passive and inert, trapped within an institutional framework in which their cognition is dominated and/or perpetually constrained. 4. Like the theory-centred approach, the institution centred approach oversimplifies human behaviour and cognition.

Table 2.1 Typology of four methods comparative studies – *Continued*

	Assumptions	Strengths	Weaknesses
Agent-centred	1. Agent consciousness and intention are fundamental to human existence. 2. The ability of individuals, groups or firms to behave in rational ways is 'bounded' by limited resources, interests and knowledge, as well as by history and geography. 3. Agents have the capacity to learn. 4. Agents operate within institutional frameworks that enable as well as delimit action: institutions provide agents with the capital or resources to operate in the world at large.	1. Recognises the constraints on information collection and the limits of agents' knowledge. 2. Accepts that such constraints apply to those who research agents' actions as well as to the agents being studied. 3. Like the case-centred approach, the agent-centred approach recognises the existence of different interpretations of common concepts – it neither denies the existence of different values or institutions nor disputes the reality of conflict over meaning and interpretation. 4. Crucially, and unlike the other three models, the agent-centred approach recognises the importance of structure *and* agency for the study of human behaviour.	1. Tends to idealise choice and strategy and the significance of agents who are the objects of study. 2. In some ways, the agent centred approach is a distinctively Western conception – a focus on agents rather than an immediate focus on cultures, institutions and organisations presupposes the existence of social frameworks consistent with and/or enabling of agent action.

P₁: Agent consciousness and intention are fundamental to human existence. Agents have the capacity to conceptualise their actions, and they have reasons for acting – 'reasons that consistently inform the flow of day-to-day activities' (Giddens 1987, p. 3). Thus actions derive from the formation of intentions which are themselves the product of belief *and* conscious thought. Crucially, agents can choose amongst alternative courses of action in most situations, and could choose not to perform such actions if they wish to do so. Decisions are based on agents' knowledge of themselves, their situations and the anticipated effects of their actions. Reflexive monitoring of the self, other agents and the social and physical contexts in which agents live are central to the decision-making process. Sewell (1992, p. 21) conceptualised agency in a similar way, arguing that it 'entails an ability to co-ordinate one's actions with others and against others, to form collective projects, to persuade, to coerce, and to monitor the simultaneous effects of one's own and others' activities'. However, and as noted below, agents are rarely able to rely on perfect knowledge and information and can only be aware of some of the likely consequences of their actions. The management of risk and uncertainty are integral to agents' goals and strategies.

P₂: The ability of individuals, groups or firms to behave in rational ways is 'bounded' by limited resources, interests and knowledge, as well as by history and geography. Because agents' information processing capacities are finite and because organisations are systems that consist of multiple goals and perspectives (see March and Simon 1958, Lindblom 1959, 1965), the costs and time inherent in mobilising the resources necessary to gather sufficient information to enable actors to evaluate all possible options renders the notion of absolute rationality virtually meaningless. Decision-making processes and the search for solutions tend to encourage risk-adverse routines. Agents often use trial-and-error in a managed way to identify the most relevant information in particular circumstances and therefore develop limited numbers of seemingly viable options. And agents make decisions knowing only some of the likely consequences of their actions. In other words they 'satisfice' (March and Simon 1958, March 1981); they find satisfactory solutions that appear to deal with the problem while controlling the risks of anticipated possible adverse outcomes.

History and geography are therefore important issues when considering the decision-making process (Clark 1994). Decision-making processes developed in the initial stages of firms' growth may have profound effects on the options considered as they evolve and mature. An initial advantage, perhaps a serendipitous decision to locate in an expanding market, can be integrated into decision-making routines, thereby affecting the conditions for future success. However, in other circumstances, the path dependency implied by such routines may constrain the ability of firms to respond to unanticipated changes in market conditions. The nature and size of the sunk costs incurred by large-scale investment in particular products and methods of production and organisation may lock-in firm decision-making, making it difficult to move from one path to another.

P_3: *Agents have the capacity to learn.* Individuals have a demonstrated ability to detect changes in circumstances and to develop a range of responses in order to modify unsuccessful behaviour (single-loop learning). Rules of action and standard operating procedures are often developed so that decisions are made in relation to some reference point. Agents tend to be less willing or capable of questioning more basic shared beliefs (double-loop learning). Instead, because of the complexity involved in social processes and because of the range of possible unanticipated outcomes inherent in decision-making, they often rely on precedents and routinised action-oriented procedures. More significantly, the questioning of fundamental assumptions can sometimes generate or give added support to powerful organisational defence mechanisms that bind agents to the past: empirically, agents are often uncomfortable with change in unstructured or ambiguous situations (Argyris 1990, Morgan 1997). Even so, considerable evidence has emerged suggesting that individuals and firms can learn to learn (Amin 1999, Argyris and Schön 1996). Many of the constraints on learning may be due to the underlying assumptions of management practice with its focus on goals, objectives and targets: 'part of the challenge [of learning] hinges on adopting an appropriate management philosophy that views and encourages the capacity of learning to learn as a key priority. It also rests on encouraging organisational principles and designs that can support this process' (Morgan 1997, p. 100).

Does this mean that agents can imitate others' *best* actions and practices? The concept of best practice is widely contested in comparative studies, and is arguably more prevalent now as competition between firms assumes an increasingly global dimension (Meiksins and Smith 1996). Best practice can be applied to ways of managing and organising as well as to broader institutional arrangements such as financial systems and structures of ownership and control. Typically, they come from societies which have achieved acknowledged positions of economic hegemony and are viewed (and often promoted) as universal cures for nominally less successful countries. In the 1980s, for instance, when the Japanese economy was outperforming its European and North American counterparts, Japanese management practices such as lean production, JIT and TQM were 'copied' by firms throughout the Western world. Such developments have led to predictions that all market-based economies will eventually converge upon a universal mode of organisation with singular methods of management and organisation (compare with Crouch and Streeck 1997).

However, local institutional arrangements may inhibit the development and diffusion of best practice. Institutions may have to transfigure to accommodate new arrangements. In practice, both of these eventualities are usually evident. The adoption of new concepts and practices may occur in large-scale systems, despite initial resistance and limited accommodation (Clark 2003). In other circumstances, local preferences or norms may be sufficiently strong to prevent 'best practices' from being adopted or may render such adoption wholly inappropriate (Gertler 2001).

P_4: *Agents operate within institutional frameworks that enable as well as delimit action.* Social processes cannot be reduced to the unconfined actions of agents. We accept the notion that just as agents create institutions, agents are also formed within and through institutions and other social processes. By this account, however, institutions are dynamic rather than static; the product of social behaviour and interaction. Some institutional economists argue against the ability of agents to knowingly change institutions and other social structures because of the complexity of social order and the unintended and unpredictable consequences of action. The agent-centred model assumes, on the other hand, that actors have the capacity to deliberately change institutions even if outcomes may be other than intended. We know this to be true because we can point to many instances where institutions have been transformed by intended action.

In addition to markets, states and systems of governance, cultural values and norms, ways of thinking and types of behaviour can be considered as kinds of institutions. Institutions are fundamental to the existence and operation of firms but also constrain their effectiveness. It is this tension which provides the impetus for institutions to change and develop over time. In other words, agents are not passive nor prisoners of their environments: their actions may be shaped by institutional imperatives just as they may shape the ways in which institutions evolve. Assuming individuals are conscious beings that have the capacity to think, learn, act and interact, we must assume that they can consider critically the society to which they belong. The implication is that they understand, at least in some general or abstract sense, the kinds of action needed to engender purposeful change as well as some of the limits of such action. Agents must also draw on their ability to persuade, coerce, motivate and lead. The agent-centred approach does not deny the very real sense in which institutions can evolve from the unintended consequences of human action. We are simply arguing that agents can and do challenge institutional structures.

Agents and institutional behaviour

In the previous section, we set out the basic assumptions underpinning our model of comparative studies. These assumptions are actually about human capacity, arguing for recognition of the importance of reflection, learning and planning – cognitive skills that we believe are universal even if their specific forms may vary between cultures and economies (Bratman 1987). Inevitably, we may be accused of 'foundationalism' or worse, recognising that these assumptions deliberately abstract from the rich texture of local circumstances. Even announcing these assumptions goes against the grain of some contemporary social theorising, especially that associated with post-modernism (Gibson and Graham 1996). So be it.

There are also some significant analytical problems hidden behind these assumptions. Most particularly, there remain important issues to be resolved concerning the relationship between agents and institutions. We begin by privileging agents in relation to institutions, even if institutions may significantly affect agents' options and choices.[6] In doing so, there is a danger that our model is in practice indistinguishable from the institution-centred model of comparative studies. In effect, the only real difference between the two models may be that when forced to make a choice between agents and institutions we would side with agents whereas institutionalists would side with institutions. Otherwise, when setting out an empirical strategy and then interpreting the data derived, both the agent-centred and the institution-centred approaches to comparative studies would effectively come to the same conclusion: institutions matter (just as history and geography matter).

One way of distinguishing between our approach and the institution-centred approach may be to consider the issue of autonomy. At the limit, our agents would or should have the option to walk away from institutional imperatives. By contrast, the institution-centred model of comparative studies implies a degree of 'capture' at odds with individual autonomy. But, of course, movement between countries is less common than might be theoretically expected, just as capture seems to be too strong a notion given the ambiguity and fluidity of institutional boundaries and borders. One way to proceed, therefore, is to treat institutions as resource endowments. In other words, we could imagine that institutions provide agents with the capital or resources (physical, social, and intellectual) to operate in the world at large (Hollis 1996). And, we could also imagine that different regions with different institutions have varying resource endowments that then affect in demonstrable ways agents' decision-making and actions (see Chapter 3).

This is a useful way forward, and a means of conceptualising the relationship between agents and institutions relevant to contemporary economic circumstances. It can accommodate arguments by social theorists and comparative analysts that social capital is a very important component of civil society affecting, for example, the allocation of risk between economic agents and institutions (Coleman 1990). Likewise, it would be a useful way of understanding the economic and geographical effects of European integration and globalisation. After all, it is apparent that agents in the same industries but located in different countries characterised by rather different cultural and social traditions seem to respond to common economic imperatives using the different instruments at their disposal. Furthermore, this kind of approach would allow us to conceptualise competition between regions and nations with regard to global competitiveness.

It has been widely recognised that resource endowments are an important way of conceptualising the role of institutions in the global economy (Storper and Salais 1997). But as a means of distinguishing between an agent-centred as opposed to an institution-centred approach to comparative studies, it also leaves open a number of possibilities. For instance, it does not resolve the question of agent autonomy. This kind of logic would work even if agents had very limited cognitive capacities; indeed, one could imagine this kind of logic working if agents had no independent ability or scope for decision-making. At the same time, if agents were completely autonomous there would seem to be little in the way of limits on agents' flexibility (as in Jensen 1998). If regions and nations were differentiated one from the other according to their resource endowments what would stop agents migrating to those places that had the 'best' resource endowments with respect to global competitiveness? One answer to this question may simply be history: until recently national citizenship has been a basic impediment to switching between countries. Also, it is as obvious in Europe as elsewhere, that language and culture remain vital (albeit informal) ingredients of citizenship.

The next step in this argument must be to attribute to agents their own resource endowments so as to assert their flexibility. To illustrate, imagine that two agents exist, each located in different regions (and countries) but affiliated with the same industry facing much the same competitive circumstances. Let us imagine that by happenstance or by design both regions have the same institutional resource endowments. But now let us imagine that one agent has more capital than the other. To make this example work all we have to assume is that the agent with more capital uses that resource in such a way that they gather better information about competitive circumstances and hence make more appropriate decisions about competitive strategy. At the end of the story that agent 'wins' over the other agent, notwithstanding the fact that they are located in nominally equivalent places. To take the example one step further, imagine that the regions can be differentiated one from the other according to their resource endowments. In this case, let us assume that the agent with the fewest individual resources is also the agent located in the region with the fewest institutional resources. The end of the story is obvious.

This simple example provides us with an analytical logic that can differentiate between agents and institutions and between agents with different institutional settings. To illustrate, Figure 2.1 summarises the interaction between agents and institutions using a familiar 2 by 2 matrix structure. Each cell of the matrix (1–4) is designed to represent a distinctive agent-institutional environment. Cell (1) is an environment in which agents' own endowments are in some sense matched by their institutional endowments, providing agents with a degree of competitive flexibility and choice of strategy that is unrivalled compared to the other three environments. Opportunism could be thought to characterise agents in this setting, using their own and institutional resources to claim market position regionally, nationally and globally. Cell (2) may be thought to be an environment in which institutional endowments in some way compensate for agents' own low resource endowments. These agents are unlikely to migrate. But they may also face a very harsh competitive environment mediated by the opportunities provided by their home region. Cell (3) could be thought to be an environment in which low institutional resources may encourage agents with high resource endowments to defect from either the rules and regulations characterising that region or the region itself. Moving between regions and countries may be one response by such agents, just as they may take advantage of higher tiers of policy institutions. Cell (4) summarises the situation in which agents are basically captured in a low resource environment.

| | | Agent Endowment | |
		High	*Low*
Institution	*High*	(1) Opportunism	(2) Enable
Endowment	*Low*	(3) Defection	(4) Capture

Figure 2.1   A typology of agent-institution interaction

Recognising its summary nature and simplicity, a number of implications follow from this analysis and typology. In the first instance, it should be apparent that an agent-centred approach to comparative study can be differentiated from an institution-centred approach by virtue of the cognitive capacities and endowments attributed to agents. In the second instance, it should also be apparent that an institutional environment characterised by relatively significant resource endowments can compensate for agent impoverishment. However, this does not mean that such institutions would overwhelm cognitive capacity. Rather, the issue here is the extent to which agents are able to act on their interests given their resources in relation to competitors' resources. In the third instance, we would accept that there is considerable scope for agent-institution interaction. For example, the idea that institutions could compensate for agent impoverishment presupposes the existence of common interests joining agents and institutions with regard to their collective place in the global economy. Finally, we would also recognise the possibility that some agents may have the cognitive capacity, resources and interest to move from their inherited institutional context. Loyalty may be a fragile moral sentiment just as the concept of 'embeddedness' may neglect the capacity of agents to understand the world of which they are part (see Chapter 4).

Limits of comparative research

In the previous discussion, we sought to identify commonalities that should guide comparative analysis. In doing so, however, we are mindful of Susan Strange's (1997) criticism of those methods of comparative study that see only the differences between regions and nations notwithstanding the logic of capitalism. Here we are less concerned with the functions of markets and the imperatives driving capitalist accumulation – in the interests of clarity we have left these issues in the background. We have sought to emphasise agent-centred issues because of their fundamental importance for understanding behaviour in both theory and practice. It is all too easy to lose touch with these issues when advocating the significance of difference between places and their institutional frameworks (witness the literature on the embedded firm; see

Grabher 1993). However, we do not wish to idealise our model of comparative studies. It seems that as practitioners of comparative studies we ought to be more mindful of the limits of such research. In this section, limits to comparative studies are identified. We begin with what we term as information constraints on comparative studies before turning to the crucial problem of translating complex concepts between languages and societies.

It is obvious that we all face constraints on the collection of information, the processing of that information into usable knowledge, and the assessment of the veracity of that knowledge. We never have enough knowledge nor do we always know the value of the knowledge that we have; we typically have to act (whether making inferences about behaviour or actually making decisions) in the face of considerable uncertainty. Of course, one objective of comparative study is to increase our stock of information while assessing the information gathered against our inherited understanding of related circumstances. Another objective of comparative study is to test expectations against new or changed circumstances in the hope of clarifying existing uncertainties. If this is important to comparative studies, it is also important to the objects of our study (agents), who are continually required to contemplate what they know in relation to the available options for action. We would argue that comparative studies must take seriously these limits faced by economic agents, as we must look carefully at what we can or cannot conclude from our research.

The Carnegie School clearly assumed that rationality is bounded by information and cognitive constraints. This does not mean that analysts such as Simon presumed people act irrationally. Rather it is assumed that people undertake action in a deliberate fashion recognising the prospect of mistakes and failures. They make decisions in the context of the available information and knowledge, recognising that both are the products of agents' interaction with immediate circumstances and changing circumstances. Comparative studies face exactly the same dilemma. Practitioners are driven by much the same imperatives with the same kinds of constraints. We cannot expect that an agent-centred approach to comparative studies can avoid such limits on knowledge. But we would also contend that the other three models of comparative studies are similarly compromised.

In addition, there remains a basic conundrum: all comparative study seems to involve the transfer of concepts between circumstances, their translation into local vernacular, and some kind of adjudication about their meanings in different circumstances. Recognising this conundrum is a necessary step when applying cross-country quantitative and qualitative research programmes. We mention cross-country research programmes because we wish to emphasise that the translation of concepts across societies is intimately connected to the language and customs of linguistic expression often associated with national and regional borders. This issue could be equally a question of comparing between regions and localities, particularly if those communities bring with them certain histories of language and expression. Whereas we are particularly sensitive to this topic, just as case-centred approaches to comparative studies are sensitive to this topic, theory-centred approaches to comparative studies simply assume the issue away by reference to a universal grammar. We do not believe that this presumption is plausible. On the other hand, we would readily recognise that it is very contentious in cognitive science (see the extensive review and analysis provided by Cowie 1999).

It is at this point that the virtues of a case-centred approach to comparative studies are most apparent. There is a deeply held presumption that case-centred approaches take seriously differences between societies as evident in the meanings ascribed to observed objects, and the possibility of rival and even different concepts. So, for example, it could be argued that a complex concept such as 'trust' means something different in the Anglo-American world where legal devices such as contract often stand in place of social custom when compared to continental European (particularly German and Italian), Japanese or Chinese business networks. While this concept is shared between social theorists in these countries, it could be argued that in many respects its meaning varies between circumstances just as its significance must be judged from rather different reference points in different countries. We need ethnographers and anthropologists to excavate the meaning of such concepts before we join them up with the theoretical architecture of the new economic geography attributed to theorists such as Krugman, Scott, and Storper (see Clark et al. 2000a for a comprehensive overview and introduction).

Even so, recognising the existence of different interpretations of common concepts and, perhaps, the existence of rival concepts is not quite the same as retreating to a case-centred approach to comparative studies. In this respect, we assert that there are at least three possible responses to such a conundrum. We could assume, just as many cognitive scientists and linguists assume, that agents use all kinds of formal and informal bridging mechanisms between themselves in order to promote mutual understanding. This does not mean that the meaning of concepts need converge to a single meaning; quite the contrary, witness the debate in Europe about the meaning of concepts such as markets and societies (Clark 2001). Rather, the use of bridging mechanisms suggests that people find ways of co-existing and casts doubt on the proposition that there are profound boundaries between cultures that prevent mutual knowledge and understanding. Furthermore, from an agent-centred perspective, we assume that people from different circumstances share similar cognitive capacities even if they do not share the same information or institutional contexts. And finally, we would argue that the imperatives underpinning capitalism are much the same everywhere. They may take different forms, and they may take different linguistic expressions. But these imperatives provide a significant bridge between circumstances (Strange 1997).

While we recognise that comparative studies are a problematic enterprise, we are sceptical of claims that societies co-exist in ways that bar the prospect of conceptual bridge building. These conceptual devices may derive from the volition of individual agents seeking ways of communicating across circumstances and places; just as common economic circumstances may provide bridging concepts by virtue of shared economic imperatives. Our view on this matter neither denies the existence of different values and institutions nor disputes the reality of conflict over meaning and interpretation.

Conclusions

In this chapter, we have sought to provoke the re-opening of the debate about the proper methods of comparative study. The chapter documents three models of comparative research, and we have sought to assess these models in relation to their apparent shortcomings. So, for example, those that advocate a theory-centred approach to comparative studies seem to make heroic assumptions about the possibility of a universal language of economic theory shared by analysts if not those who are the objects of comparative analyses. At the same time, we are sceptical about the plausibility of case-centred approaches to comparative studies. As Western culture seeps into the most remote corners of human life, the idealism implied by the case-centred approach appears increasingly archaic. Likewise, we are not particularly enthusiastic about the new institutional approaches of economics, geography and sociology: they tend to marginalise the role of agents in the formation of institutions. In our agent-centred approach, we emphasise the importance of grounding comparative studies by reference to basic assumptions about human cognitive, behavioural, and reflexive capacities.

It might be argued that our agent-centred approach to comparative studies is a distinctively Western conception. We would accept that focus on agents as opposed to focus upon cultures, institutions and organisations presupposes the existence of social frameworks consistent with and/or enabling of agent action. And we would also accept that agent-focused comparative studies presupposes that agents have resources from which to execute their plans. One should not idealise choice and strategy. We would accept any claim to the effect that when agents are trapped within institutional regimes antithetical to agent action our analytical focus (and its internal logic) may be less relevant than we have intimated. But we would not accept, in this context, any case-specific argument which asserted that such agents are so dominated by institutional imperatives that they are unreflexive and non-cognitive (being simply and solely the bearers of institutional structures). There is a danger embedded in both the case-specific approach to comparative studies and in the new institutional approach to comparative studies of *structure without agency*.

Furthermore, we would argue that globalisation threatens the integrity of any regime which supposes that their institutional imperatives should remain dominant and exclusive. Even so, we should acknowledge that of the three models surveyed and criticised above, our approach to comparative studies is most consistent with new institutional approaches. We accept that the interaction between agents and institutions is an important element in understanding competitive (community, regional and national) responses to the forces of globalisation. Moreover, we have emphasised that agents' information, knowledge, and cognitive skills may have systematic impacts on local outcomes when combined with varying levels of resource endowment. In this regard, institutional capacity could be seen as a means of empowering agent action just as institutional incapacity and constraints could be seen as barriers to agents' behaviour. Ultimately, local variations in agents' actions in relation to common issues (like global industrial competition) could be, in part, attributed to institutional characteristics. Local 'success' in the global economy may be a matter of competition between local systems of economic and political governance and the extent to which those systems affect agents' actions.

So let us not idealise agents' actions or comparative studies. In the penultimate section of the chapter we emphasised that there may well be limits to comparative studies – limits that are related to agents' cognitive capacities and the effectiveness of bridging mechanisms which enable mutual understanding. There is an intricate argument embedded in this point; it has to do with the role and status of complex concepts in human understanding. Drawing upon debates in linguistics and psychology, we suggested that the process of conceptualising one's place in relation to globalisation (for example) relies upon informal and formal bridging mechanisms aimed at integrating understanding. When concepts are formed at the local level out of an inherited stock of related concepts, there is a danger that bridging mechanisms will fail to adequately accommodate the distinctive history of otherwise apparently similar notions. Because of resource constraints, it seems inevitable that trial and error experiments designed to enhance mutual understanding could fall short of a true understanding of overlapping circumstances.

Most importantly, the existence of such limits jointly affects both the agents who are the subjects of analysis and those who research agents' actions. One peculiar feature of comparative studies is the presumption that those who are the objects of analysis have bounded (local) consciousness whereas those who study those agents have at least a higher order (external) consciousness or even a universal consciousness that allows for independent scrutiny. Social science is as much affected by the uncertain status of concepts as we suppose that agents are affected by their local context. If we are unable to form some kind of bridge between similar concepts, comparative studies risks becoming little more than inconclusive dialogue. Theory can play a crucial role in sustaining dialogue and in at least partly overcoming the translation problem. Even so, social science theory and practice must begin from a particular vantage point in history and geography. To think otherwise would be to re-invent a gross caricature of social knowledge that seems to have finally been recognised for what it is – a fabrication rather than a reality.

3
Path Dependence and Development

National systems of accumulation and regulation are vulnerable to mobile capital and international competition in local product markets. Debate rages, however, over the implications to be drawn from such observations. For some, capital mobility threatens cultural and linguistic traditions being a potent force of homogenisa tion. For others, capital mobility is vastly exaggerated being, more often than not, held in check by persistent national and regional traditions (Dicken 2000). For some, the nation-state epitomises the remarkable achievements of social democracy being the most appropriate scale for managing markets and protecting the welfare of those vulnerable to corrosive forces of market competition (Streeck 1997). For others, more ambivalent about 20th century history, market competition may have the virtue of disrupting local coalitions in the interests of European consumers.

As European economic integration proceeds, these issues have apparent increasing theoretical and practical significance. For those concerned about the role and competitive status of regions in Europe, the current balance of argument favours those who believe that persistent geographical diversity under-pins European development (Antonelli 2001). By this logic, local traditions as represented by industrial districts, craft and occupational associations, networks and relationships, and indigenous capital resources will sustain endogenous regional growth alongside the expanding geographical scope and penetration of Europe's largest companies. Theoretically, a wide array of related conceptual tools have been invoked to sustain this argument including spatial complementarities (Porter

2000), embeddedness (Grabher 1993), social capital (Coleman 1990) and relational capital (Bathelt and Glückler 2000), untraded dependencies (Storper and Salais 1997) and most importantly path dependence, increasing returns and the lock-in phenomenon (Arthur 1994). See also Scott (1998) for a statement about spatially differentiated global economic growth.

In this chapter, we re-consider the virtues of path dependence. In doing so, we build upon our agent-centred approach outlined in the previous chapter which provides for reflexivity and learning. Here, our model allows for local embeddedness but also the possibility of defection whether tacit or active. Economic agents are assumed to be neither prisoners of the past or of a particular jurisdiction, nor are they assumed unencumbered with respect to their strategic (economic and geographical) options. We also return to the issue of European market diversity, and its argued persistence in the face of the global forces driving towards convergence in form and function (see Crouch and Streeck 1997). It should be noted that our approach is, more often than not, conceptual and argumentative. We use abstraction to expand the range of possibilities in economic geography.

The chapter begins with a critical assessment of Arthur's (1994) seminal model of path dependence and regional development. This leads on to issues of contingency and rationality inspired by Simon (1956, 1997). Whereas *contingency* is a very useful and powerful analytical tool, we also recognise that agents know about and have an interest in seeing outside the local environment. Indeed, an important attribute of successful decision-making is the process of winnowing out or selecting amongst the available market information in the light of agents' strategic goals. These ideas can be attributed to the early work of Keynes (1921) and Knight (1921). Taking these insights further, however, we suggest that agents rely heavily upon their *inheritance* and *endowments* (firm-specific and social, local and national, etc) to evaluate their options in the light of market conditions. It is shown that local endowments may enable decision-making and even promote agents' best interests. But endowments may constrain and even neutralise agents' decision-making capacities. In a *multi-jurisdictional environment* like the European Union, the nature and scope of local endowment may be a vital ingredient in understanding how and why some agents stay in place and contribute to local growth whereas others defect and contribute to regional decline (Whitley 2000).

At the outset, it should be acknowledged that our analysis violates canonical assumptions of conventional economic analysis. Like Krugman (1991), our point of departure is an assessment of how and why multiple equilibria may persist in space and time (compare with Bicchieri 1993). We do not invoke hard-and-fast rules about the necessity of rationality compared, for example, with Jensen (1998) who presupposes the dominance of maximisation behaviour. Rather, our argument about agents' decision-making exploits a metaphor Gigerenzer and Selten (2001, 4) attributed to Herbert Simon (1956): that behaviour can be characterised as 'a pair of scissors, where one blade is the "cognitive limitations" of actual humans and the other the "structure of the environment". Minds with limited time, knowledge, and other resources can be nonetheless successful by exploiting structures in their environments'. In our case, we suggest that the local environment can be divided into inherited assets and liabilities and the flow of income (endowment) that may be derived from an inherited asset. This logic allows for environments that are liability traps, for environments characterised by the short-term discounting of inherited assets through immediate consumption, and for environments remarkably different from the other not withstanding nominally similar or equal amounts of inheritance.

Regional differentiation

The notion of path dependence is an often-observed phenomenon: the persistence of local customs and traditions differentiating one place from another. For economic geographers, it combines history and geography in a formal fashion thereby providing analytical justification for the working assumptions underpinning the discipline. By contrast, much of neo classical economics presumes the existence of self-correcting mechanisms that strip away differences between places, the end result being a single and unique equilibrium across the whole economy. By this logic, convergence in economic form and function is characteristic of modern capitalist economies driving out systematic differences between localities and regions in the face of common market imperatives (Barro and

Sala-I-Martin 1995). Once recognised, the concept of path dependence has been rapidly incorporated into economics (see Antonelli 1997), economic geography (Clark, Feldman and Gertler 2000), and related disciplines including political science and sociology (see Crouch and Streeck 1997), as well as comparative corporate governance and law (see, for example, Bebchuk and Roe 1999).

According to Arthur (1994), path dependence is actually the product of two inter-related and reinforcing processes: positive feedback as represented by increasing returns to scale, and the lock-in process whereby economic agents remain with particular paths of accumulation notwithstanding the alternatives. These are hardly original empirical observations. For example, writers such as Kaldor and Myrdal discussed similar ideas of cumulative causation and regional differentiation in incomes and employment (see generally Clark, Gertler and Whiteman 1986). Likewise, early work by Curry (1998) suggested that, beginning from an arbitrarily assigned economic location, there are systematic and reinforcing economic processes that would result in highly differentiated maps of economic activity. Arthur's remarkable contribution was to synthesise these ideas into an analytically tractable and comprehensive explanation of the existence of multiple equilibria.

For many theorists, the virtues of path dependence are readily apparent. Increasing returns to scale reward prior decisions to invest in certain production technologies and locations while promising further rewards for remaining loyal to the accumulated configuration of production. The effectiveness of market arbitrage processes are muted by virtue of a further assumption that learning-by-doing provides incumbent firms with path-specific knowledge for best exploiting increasing returns not easily replicated by rival firms located elsewhere or by those firms that would wish to enter closely related markets. If we add one further complication, the existence of place-specific knowledge embodied in certain distinctive local (national or regional) customs and practices, then we can provide an analytical argument that explains observed reality. For example: the persistence of industrial districts based upon local relations not easily reproduced elsewhere (Cooke and Morgan 1998), and the problems encountered by multi-jurisdictional firms in applying technologies developed in one place to other places within the same firm (Gertler 2001).

The theory of path dependence suggests that various local firms and industries come to depend upon increasing returns, spreading-out from 'core' firms via accumulated external and agglomeration economies. In earlier work, Kaldor (1970) showed that a firm's productivity may have a significant 'local' growth component adding to whatever internal factors may contribute to observed firm-specific productivity and real wages (Verdoorn's law). This kind of argument has been re-worked in recent years by reference to the positive affects for regional economic growth of spin-offs, networks, and technological spillovers, providing a rationale for the endogenous growth of industry-regions such as Silicon Valley, Rt128/495 (Boston) and Oxfordshire (UK). If, however, core firms encounter progressive limits on increasing returns, and if they begin to encounter rival firms-regions with competing profiles in home markets, lock-in could gradually stifle innovation and perhaps pre-cipitate a switch from positive to negative feedback. Increasing returns encourages specialisation, indeed may rely upon specialisa-tion to sustain competitiveness; hence the prospect of being vulner-able to unanticipated *and* anticipated non-local structural shifts in external market conditions (Radner and Stiglitz 1984).

The threat behind lock-in is homogeneity. As core elements of an industry-region growth complex come to dominate economic life, local social and political institutions may come to rely upon its income and opportunities. Existing social and political institutions may respond to the core interests of the local economy using its resources to reinforce the lock-in process. Consequently, global competitive pressures may be met by resistance: institutional sclero-sis and non-adaptation, a failure or refusal to learn, copy, and adapt to the elements of successful competing models, or a rate of change which is too slow relative to other industry-region models. Economic integration often means a new *level* of competition that penalises incremental path-dependent adaptation. Therefore, the mutual co-existence of different systems of accumulation could be replaced with once-and-for-all knockout tournaments that result in the survival of one 'model' at the expense of others. As Arthur has noted, the costs of slow response in such circumstances may vary significantly just as the costs of exit may accumulate to the point where whole industry-regions are undermined. In circum-stances where social and political institutions are implicated in the accumulated configuration of production, economic restructuring may be heavily politicised (Clark and Wrigley 1997).

Nevertheless, too much can be made of lock-in and path dependence. There is a temptation to assign to individual agents a common share in the putative benefits of positive feedback as if the industry-region is representative of all agents, all interests, and all customs and traditions. In many cases, there is ample evidence of unrelated economic activities co-existing with the core elements of successful industry-region complexes. Furthermore, recognising the risks of being over-invested in one model of economic growth, even core agents may have an interest in diversifying their potential choices and opportunities. For that matter, who would suggest that local social and political institutions are so hegemonic that defection and dissent are washed away by the possible (transitory) success of one path of accumulation?

Contingency and rationality

In suggesting that economic agents may look outside local circumstances and institutions to a world of competing models and competing market players we have returned to basic assumptions made in previous chapters about the scope of agents' cognitive capacities and knowledge. Before developing these arguments in more detail, we should look more closely at the related behavioural assumptions of Arthur's (1994) theory of path dependence.

It is difficult to summarise Arthur's model of the relationship between agents and institutions. In part, this is because he weaves together a variety of claims about rationality at different points in his argument in favour of a comprehensive picture of regional differentiation. For example, he begins by criticising neo-classical economics for its obsession with single and unique equilibrium. To sustain this criticism, he explains behaviour by the rewards of increasing returns and notes the implication that so-called non-optimal technologies may persist in certain geographical and historical circumstances against expectations to the contrary (quoting, for example, Paul David 1985 and the QWERTY case; see also Foray 1997). Further into his argument, he invokes a version of bounded rationality to explain why 'spatial order is process-dependent' (focusing upon the circumstantial constraints *imposed* on rational-

ıty). In a similar vein, he devotes considerable attention to the interaction between chance and necessity. Serial and spatial autocorrela-
tion is both an explanation and an elaboration of historical
dependence.

Theoretically, Arthur is balanced on a knife-edge; on one side are
the absurd assumptions of neo-classical economics while on the
other side there are the dangers of *ad hoc* historical and geographical
reasoning. In between, is a theory of rationality with two prongs:
(1) a simple signal-response model of behaviour, augmented by (2) a
more complicated learning-by-doing model of behaviour that provides a rationale for serial-dependence. While he mentions bounded
rationality, he does not reference Herbert Simon. His theoretical perspective is more consistent with Stigler (1961) and Spence's (1981)
models of signalling, search and information acquisition. Explicitly
referenced is a theory of rational expectations and behaviour constrained by the costs of information acquisition. By virtue of the
first prong, increasing returns are rewards fully integrated into
agents' expectations and subsequent behaviour. By virtue of the
second prong, learning-by-doing exploits an initial advantage
thereby reinforcing expectations and commitment to the region-
specific path of accumulation. Arthur takes as given 'globally' heterogeneous but 'locally' homogeneous market signals in contrast to
neo-classical economics that assumes a world of common information consistent with a global steady-state.

Consider the implications of his model. For economic agents on
the upwards-sloping curve of positive feedback, their response to
market signals combined with the response of other similarly
located economic agents provides for a system of reinforcing mutual
advantage. To the extent that local economic development relies
upon intensive networks of exchange and the trade in complementary expertise, private information is diffused through social relationships. In a local sense, economic activity is pareto-optimal;
theoretically and empirically economic agents following their interests undertake exchange according to the ranked relative costs and
benefits of each transaction. Inevitably, norms and customs develop
which codify such expectations. Over time, these norms and
customs may provide institutional mechanisms for monitoring and
enforcing expectations. This may be entirely positive. But as we
have seen over the past decade, region-specific mutually reinforcing

expectations may be diffused from one region through the whole economy becoming a financial boom, bubble and bust. Irrational exuberance may replace rational expectations (see especially Shiller 2000 on the TMT phenomenon).

Consider also the implications of this model for agents whose activities are *off the curve* of positive feedback although resident in a region dominated by agents *on the curve*. In such a dual economy, there would be no incentive for on the curve agents to transact with off the curve agents. They would be isolated, economically and socially. There may be, of course, an external industry-specific as opposed to region-specific path of accumulation that local agents could join. This would be mediated by the costs of transportation and communication (distance) as well as the costs of information acquisition and evaluation (making sense of market signals). Such spatially elongated production systems exist across the globe; not every industry is organised as a spatial cluster (compare Clark 1993 with Porter 2000). But doing so often requires significant agent-specific financial resources. Common local resources like external and agglomeration economies would be irrelevant to the particular needs of off the curve economic agents. So there seems to be no reason for off the curve economic agents to persist with their activities. With all the positive incentives, what would stop them from joining the dominant opportunity set? Alternatively, what would stop them from leaving the jurisdiction for another with an opportunity set more consistent with their plans and aspirations?

To summarise, there are three troubling implications that derive from Arthur's behavioural assumptions. In the first instance, it seems inevitable that regions become more specialised over time. This is either because the unrelated activities off the curve of positive feedback are 'taken-over' by on the curve economic agents or because agents in unrelated activities are forced to flee such jurisdictions. This may be true of some regions but many other regions seem persistently diverse. In the second instance, it seems that there are no limits to mutually reinforcing expectations. This is troubling because it presages speculative bubbles about the expected flow of increasing returns, as well as catastrophic crashes when expectations are not fulfilled. In the third instance, his model implies that social capital is derivative or functionally designed rather than inherited.

Region-specific social capital is presumably flexible in that it is designed and redesigned in accordance with those on the curve of positive feedback as opposed to those off the curve. Finally, it would seem that region-specific social capital is quite homogeneous given the dominance of on the curve activities.

Inheritance and endowment

The previous exercise in logic reflects Arthur's behavioural assumptions about the nature of rationality. One consequence is a world in which history and geography are merely accumulated constraints, incentives and opportunities rather than inherited institutions and practices. This may be appropriate if the intellectual project is explaining the rise of Silicon Valley and the like (see also Saxenian 1994). Whatever its separate regional histories and trajectories, there is, at least, a common US institutional framework over-arching and under-pinning a map of diverse economic and financial resources. But in the European context, this is surely implausible and a heavily contested ideal. Whatever the imperatives driving European economic integration, it is obvious that diverse national and regional institutions and practices are inherited rather simply accumulated as a by-product of growth and development.

In this section, we re-consider history and geography by referencing two related concepts: inheritance and endowment. This is the basis for explaining how and why agent decision-making may have a significant environmental (historical and geographical) component without reducing agent action to just the context or environment in which agents find themselves (Simon 1956). As all agents are located at a point in time and space, we assume that agents inherit from their families, communities and societies (respectively) *property, resources, obligations and entitlements.* Agents' inheritance may be well-defined real property and objects. Agents may also inherit community resources like public infrastructure as well as less formal community resources like customs and norms (social capital). At the national and EU levels, agents may be thought to inherit the obligations and entitlements of national citizenship. Inheritance is an unearned transfer of assets, entitlements, and institutions from one generation to another (perhaps in the form of a social contract).

Inheritance – assets and liabilities

It is tempting to treat inheritance as if it is always valuable. But there is an important issue of relevance: the extent to which that which is inherited from the past (time t–1) is relevant to current circumstances (time t) and expected circumstances (time t+1). To illustrate, an agent may inherit a firm from his/her parents, s/he may inherit certain community resources like a network of contacts and commitments, and s/he may inherit a certain competitive place in the local and European economy. If the firm is under-capitalised, if the local network is impoverished, and if the local economy subject to intensive competition any inheritance may be a liability rather than an asset. Further more, an inheritance may carry with it certain obligations to the past and to the community limiting agents' discretion and strategic capacities. For instance, they may inherit a certain 'place' in the local economy and be committed by virtue of their assumed obligations to sustaining the past notwithstanding its apparent lack of economic competitiveness (inside and outside of the region).

Let us be more systematic. With reference to Figure 3.1, assume that there are three types of inherited assets from the family (e.g. a small firm), community (e.g. local networks and relationships), and nation (e.g. rules and regulations regarding competition). Assume that these closely related inherited assets existed prior to our representative economic agent, and that our economic agent is unable to affect their value at least in the short term. To sustain our case, we also assume that the value of any inheritance can be classified as positive (enabling action and decision-making), neutral (providing no impediments to action), or negative (limiting or constraining desired actions and decision-making). To illustrate, an economic agent may inherent a highly capitalised small firm with strong reinforcing community networks and an advantageous location in national and international markets. In effect, our economic agent may be lucky enough (for the moment) to be a second-generation TMT entrepreneur located in Silicon Valley. With respect to Figure 3.1, we would identify this type of situation as Case One (as opposed to Case Two immediately above).

However, there are many more possibilities. Take for example, Case Three. In this situation, our economic agent inherits from the family a firm with sufficient economic resources to be competitive,

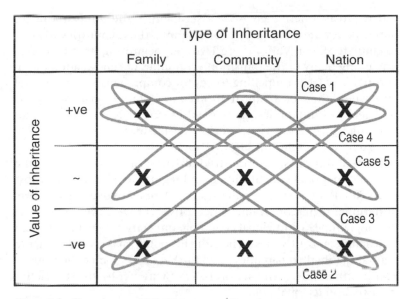

Figure 3.1 Taxonomy of Inheritance, and its value to economic agents

located in a region perhaps best characterised as benignly co-operative, but impeded by a national regulatory framework that limits or restricts the capacity of our agent to take advantage of inherited circumstances to reach out into the wider economic world. Alternatively, our economic agent may inherit little in the way of family resources, but be placed in a community with very strong relational and social capital notwithstanding a neutral (at best) regulatory environment. Our economic agent may be able to take advantage of the community setting to compensate for the lack of family resources and the relative lack of opportunities provided by the national business system (Case Four). Finally, consider Case Five. In this instance, family inheritance is assumed to be entirely negative combined with little in the way of community resources but dominated by a very strong competitive national regulatory environment. This would seem to be an environment in which large firms dependent upon institutional capital dominate the regions of the nation, and compete in the global economy. In effect, small firms and community innovation may be squeezed out by centralised institutions.

If we treat inheritance as an asset-liability the implications for public policy are all too clear. For example, those countries wishing to emulate Silicon Valley (Case Two) but beginning from Case One (including many of the transition economies of central and Eastern Europe) may face compelling forces for comprehensive reform. Not only would there be an apparent need to sustain inter-generational transfers within families, there would seem to be a strong case for building-up community networks that facilitate co-operation and the exchange of relevant information along the lines suggested by analysts and theorists of industrial districts, sustained by profound reform of national constitutional and regulatory regimes. For those countries dominated by small firms in co-operative regions, reform of national regulatory frameworks consistent with the imperatives driving European and global economic integration may be sufficient to sustain competitiveness. The issue for policy makers is whether to neutralise inherited liabilities or go further and enhance the value of agents' inheritance – in part, an issue of whether to invest in active industry and regional policy.

Here, we wish to emphasise two points. First, an agent's inheritance may have profound consequences for their competitiveness and regional prosperity, although second, agents and policy makers may deliberately select, vary or ignore that which is inherited in the interests of promoting long-term economic development. See March (1994, 91–95) on the ways in which agents value the past. In part, the capacity of agents and policy makers to adapt inherited resources and institutions depends upon the availability of economic resources as well as information and knowledge about prospective opportunities. We could imagine circumstances where inherited resources and institutions are long-term traps imprisoning inadequately resourced economic agents and their communities notwithstanding a realisation that there are opportunities that could be taken advantage of in the race to sustain competitiveness. Equally, we could imagine circumstances where inherited resources and institutions reinforce existing growth trajectories. This is perhaps another way of accounting for (positive and negative) cumulative causation.

Endowment as a flow of income

We should also recognise that an agent's inheritance can be treated as an endowment if capitalised as a flow of income. In the literature, there is a tendency to treat inheritance and endowment as much the same phenomenon. But, not all inherited assets could be or should be treated as endowments. For example, economic agents may take the wealth of a family firm and convert it into consumption, they may exploit community networks and relational capital for short-term advantage, and they may use national regulatory systems against local collaborators. In part, the issue of transforming inherited assets into endowments is an issue of discounting opportunism in favour of investment. This issue is as much about expectations of the future as it is about the immediate benefits of consumption. Indeed, we could imagine circumstances where economic agents realise that past success may be soon exhausted. There may be significant incentives to convert inherited assets at risk to a pending economic crisis into non-path dependent residential property (for instance).

An endowment is an inherited asset that is invested, combining conservation of value with additional long-term benefits that go beyond the immediate value attributed to consumption. So, for example, an inherited family firm may be treated as a future flow of income subject to strategies that conserve its value over time. Likewise, community networks and relational capital may be treated as institutions to be reproduced from one time period to the next given their contribution to long-term collective competitiveness. Furthermore, a nation's regulatory regime could be thought to be an investment in the future just as it represents at any point in time a set of costs and benefits imposed upon economic agents. Notice, however, the distinction between using an inheritance in an incremental way and as an endowment shifts our analytical focus from Arthur's notion of path dependence to a more comprehensive notion of investment amongst various strategic options.

To illustrate, consider Figure 3.2. There we have summarised via a simple taxonomy the potential effects of an endowment on agents' strategic options given various investment horizons. Imagine that there are three rather different investment horizons representing different economic expectations: the short run (where anything beyond time t+1 is uncertain and heavily discounted), a contingent time horizon (where there are a viable range of possibilities beyond time t+1), and a long-term time horizon (where expectations are firmly rooted in apparent long-term structural transformation or technological innovation). On the other side are three rather different strategic options. We suggest that there is an option to exploit immediate circumstances, there is an option to use an asset as an endowment to adapt to changing circumstances, and there is an option to use an endowment to build long-term capacity. Agents may pursue, of course, all three options. And agents may use one option such as building long-term capacity to sustain other options such as adaptation and exploitation. We do not wish to over-emphasise the strength and coherence of these options. Rather, they are used to illustrate prospects and possibilities.

Figure 3.2 also provides a set of five ideal types, representing in space and time the interaction between investment horizons and strategic options. Consider, for example, Silicon Valley, which provides cumulative but short-term opportunities for agents and related networks to capitalise on the flow of income. This is, of course, Arthur's seminal case of path dependence. By contrast, Baden Wurttemberg is often characterised as dominated by long-term investment horizons sustained by long-term opportunities for agents and their networks to capitalise and recapitalise the flow of

| | | Investment Horizon | | |
		Short-run	Contingent	Long-run
Agent strategy	Exploitative	City of London	X	S. E. Asia
	Adaptive	X	Oxfordshire	X
	Cumulative	Silicon Valley	X	Baden-Württemberg

Figure 3.2   Endowment effects on agents' investment and strategy

income. These are very different economies. The former is thought dominated by competition rather than the co-operation whereas the latter is thought dominated by co-operation rather than competition (compare Saxenian 1994 with Cooke and Morgan 1998 and see Gertler 2003). At a most general level, it could be contended that the contrast drawn is between Anglo-American systems of market-based competition and continental European systems of long-term co-operative relationships designed to exploit national and international markets. Implied is a profound difference in corporate governance and the distribution of the flow of income between various stakeholders in the local economy.

Consider also the City of London in relation to Southeast Asia. In the first instance, the City of London continuously capitalises and recapitalises the past. In doing so, it exploits its place in the global economy as it exploits the immediate resources and capacities held within firms and passed between firms in the form of mobile talented labour. It does so extraordinarily quickly, and it does so without regard to past obligations and commitments. Individually and collectively, economic agents use the flow of income to exploit economic opportunities throughout the world. If there is a path of accumulation, it is a path that is always interrupted and refashioned by external events. By contrast, many regions of Southeast Asia have become the destinations for foreign direct investment being sites of long-term investment by multinational enterprises using income flows from within their portfolios of inherited assets and liabilities. Rather different is Oxfordshire, combining a contingent investment horizon (being dependent upon local technological innovation) and an adaptive competitive strategy (switching between streams of technological development). This is a most flexible region made so by the relatively small scale of economic units and the availability of local network-intensive and external venture-capital investment resources.

Europe as a multi-jurisdictional environment

In common with much of the literature devoted to regional economic analysis, our analytical logic has focused upon the distinctiveness of places. Unfortunately, and not withstanding our focus upon economic agents, by analysing agent-environment interaction in this way there is a temptation to treat both as distinctive and different from other agents and environments. Worse, if reduced to its bare bones our analytical logic could be used to justify treating economic agents as derivative of their regions or worse as prisoners of their regions. As we know, one dimension of agent strategy must be the option to switch between jurisdictions or environments suggesting the possibility that agents have a choice of location over the long term even if they must begin from a certain point in time and space. In this section, we add a third element to our analytical framework: Europe as a multi-jurisdictional environment systematically differentiated by national cultures and regulatory practices (at one level) and community networks and relationships (at a lower level in the geographical hierarchy).

Before doing so, however, we must distinguish between European and Anglo-American circumstances. Taking the United States as the reference point, many economic analysts suggest that both capital and labour have a wide variety of possible locations and the cognitive and financial resources necessary to exercise their optimal choice of location. There is a massive literature devoted to explicating and disputing this argument, drawn from neo-classical (Barro and Sala-I-Martin 1995) and not so neo-classical economic perspectives (Clark, Gertler and Whiteman 1986). This idealised map of seemingly unlimited opportunities and mobility potentials is hardly representative of European experience (Martin 2001). Even so, the past 50 years or so has seen remarkable shifts in population and employment between European sectors and regions. This is apparent in all western European countries and the member countries of the European Union as indicated by the migration of rural agricultural workers to major metropolitan centres dominated by manufacturing and advanced services. In the first instance, we concentrate on jurisdictional options within nations before going on to jurisdictional options between nations (the ideal underpinning the project of European integration and the development of the single market; see Monti 1996).

Location options within nations

To do so, consider Figure 3.3. There in a simple 2 by 2 matrix we have set the (positive or negative) value of family inheritance against the (positive or negative) value of community inheritance.

As in the previous analysis, we simply assume that an economic agent inherits from his or her family a firm (or more broadly production potential) that may or may not have immediate market value by virtue of either the nature of assets and liabilities inherited or by virtue of the particular place of the inherited firm in the market. With respect to community inheritance, we assume that some communities have high levels of social and relational capital that enable agent decision-making whereas other communities are not so blessed. Indeed, we could imagine that some communities are characterised by co-operative (win-win) relationships that sustain individual agents in local and national economies whereas some communities are characterised by zero-sum competition thereby impeding economic agents in their individual attempts to accumulate capital. That is, imagine economic agents inherit assets and liabilities from their family just as they inherit a particular location in the national economy.

Let us look at each of the four possibilities, being particular types of locations in time and space. Location (1) is particularly advantageous for our economic agent, combining positive family and

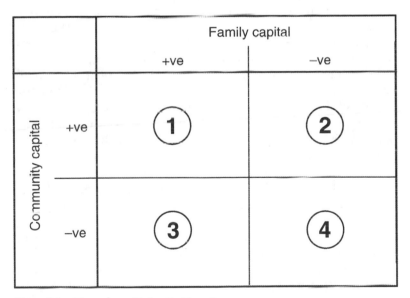

Figure 3.3 The value of inherited location

community inheritance thereby reinforcing his or her inherited location. By contrast location (4) is particularly disadvantageous for our economic agent, implying impoverishment in the short term. Over the long term, moreover, our economic agent may be unable to accumulate sufficient resources to adequately learn about other circumstances and/or move to take advantage of (for example) other communities characterised by relatively advantageous social and relational capital. In this context, the only possibility would be policy intervention in the form of the transfer of additional national resources to our economic agent (and other similarly situated agents in the community). Of course, this may simply allow our economic agent to relocate to a more appropriate environment. Notice, that our agent might consider either location (1) or location (2) assuming that there are no inter-family transfers of resources and only the shared value of community capital.

Now consider in more detail location (2) and location (3). For an economic agent that begins at location (2), a higher value of community inheritance may be sufficient to compensate for the lack of family inheritance. Indeed, to the extent to which community inheritance is capitalised as an endowment by individuals and the entire community, our economic agent may not have to contemplate a move between jurisdictions (to location 1). In the short-term, of course, our economic agent would not have sufficient resources to make such a move. But over long term, as our agent takes advantage of his or her community environment the accumulation of wealth may become an inheritance passed on into the future within the family and within the community. By contrast, an economic agent that begins in location (3) faces a much wider opportunity set. In the short term, an agent in such a location may simply spend down his or her inheritance. In the long term, if he or she were to capitalise on that inheritance and then seek an environment in which his or her endowment could be multiplied by the existence of high social and relational capital, location (1) or (2) would be certainly preferable to location (3). In this case, inherited economic resources would ameliorate information constraints on searching out the best possible location for the long-term accumulation of wealth.

We believe that this kind of logic can account for the emergence and dominance of type 1 locations in national urban systems (for example, Athens). We also believe that type 2 locations may persist over the long term notwithstanding competition from cities like Athens just as type 3 locations may persist even if they slowly decline in relative terms (their shares of population and wealth) over the long term. At the same time, this kind of logic allows for the co-existence (but rapid decline) of type 4 locations even if economic agents trapped in such locations would be, in theory at least, better off in another type of jurisdiction. Likewise, by linking family and community inheritance and endowment with the possible origins and destinations of economic agents we can show that path dependence is a dynamic and contingent process of relative location rather than a never-ending process of internal cumulative causation and local reinforcing expectations.

Location options within Europe

The next step in the analysis is to consider location options in Europe, as if there is an integrated single market for goods and services. Of course, the ideal of the single market is a long-term project, as much a political project of mutual accommodation and recognition as it is an economic project of production and consumption across geographical environments. At one level, European integration pits national systems of regulation against one another as national champions seek short-term and long-term advantage. At another level, European integration is also about the competitive potential of economic agents located in specific regions and distinguished one from the other according to their competitive capacities. In this section, we look closely at the economic and geographical implications of diverse national environments linked with variations in agent competitive capacity. This is not an exhaustive analysis so much as an indicative analysis of prospects and possibilities.

Consider Figure 3.4. There we have identified in a rather schematic fashion three different types of national environments. One is characterised as unorganised, meaning either a relatively weak state or one paralysed by conflict over economic policy such that consistent regulation is quite impossible. Another national environment is designated as role-driven indicating the dominance of a system of policy-setting and regulation which reflects and amplifies existing cultural and social hierarchies. In other words, we mean to represent a national environment in which the market is deemed secondary to existing claims on resources and relationships distributed between political and social elites. Finally, we suggest that there are national environments that are rule-driven, being regulatory frameworks designed to sustain the functions and structure of market competition. Clearly, these are gross idealisations. It would be quite difficult to match-up these ideal types with existing European nations. Indeed, if we were to consider the European Union and the European Commission we acknowledge that all three types of environments (and other unspecified types of environments) co-exist within its institutions.

On the other side of Figure 3.4 is *agent capacity*, defined as the competitive potential of economic agents nationally and internationally. Here, we draw together their family and community resources and attribute an arbitrary measure of high, medium, and low capacity. In doing so, we would suggest that a high measure of agent capacity indicates that the agent that occupies an advantageous regional location combining positive family inheritance with strong community relational capital. By contrast, we would suggest

		National environment		
		Un-organised	Role-driven	Rule-driven
Agent capacity	High	**X**		
	Medium		**X**	
	Low			**X**

Figure 3.4   Interaction between agents and national institutions

that a low measure of agent capacity indicates the agent occupies a rather disadvantageous location being dominated by impoverished family and community resources. In effect, we could imagine that all nine cells of the matrix can be attributed to a real location or region in space and time. Again it would be foolish to identify specific places in part because of our limited knowledge of the entire European map of agent circumstances.

Take for example the top left-hand corner of the matrix, high agent capacity combined with an unorganised national environment. In effect, the national regulatory environment is deemed either irrelevant or neutral for such agents suggesting a region-centred path of accumulation that may spill over into the national economy. Also suggested is a wide scope of geographical activity, going well beyond the boundaries of the agent and his or her region to the European economy at large. In this instance, regional economic growth and agent prosperity may be thought to be driven by local circumstances; in effect, suggested is an endogenous and cumulative growth engine. On the other hand, were such a region to falter (due to internal contradictions or the actions of an external competitor) it would seem that the national regulatory infrastructure could do little to impede or ameliorate its demise. In this context, the growth and transfer of wealth within the region and between economic agents could be capitalised as an endowment that flows out into the global financial economy. Furthermore, just as Silicon Valley precipitated a global speculative financial bubble so too could the collapse of such a region affect the long-term development of the national (if not global) economy.

Moving on to the second example, the cell in the middle of the matrix combines a role-driven national environment with medium agent capacity. Here, at least, agent capacity is not obviously impeded by an unorganised or chaotic national regulatory environment. On the other hand, it may not benefit as similarly situated agents may benefit from a rule-driven national regulatory environment that facilitates the competitiveness of agents and their regions in the European economy. At issue is the degree to which a role-driven policy process stifles the needed innovation of agents in their regions. This issue can be recast as one where we consider the extent to which the social structure and cultural orientation of a national polity dominates agents and their community environments. For example, existing agent capacity may be taken up in forms of social and cultural recognition that discount the long-term creation of wealth and its transfer to successive local generations (as inheritance and potential endowment). However, it should be noted that medium agent capacity could by happenstance take advantage of an institution within a role-driven national environment and make a substantial claim on European product markets.

Finally, refer to the bottom right-hand corner of the matrix. For agents and communities so situated, this is hardly a positive situation. After all, a rule-driven national environment is one that is unlikely to make an exception for distressed firms, industries or regions. Indeed, a rule-driven national environment may be to the advantage of existing national centres of international competitiveness while doing little to protect the industries and agents of depressed regions from competitors better situated in other environments. Here, there is an obvious set of examples. In the UK, characterised by a regime of regulation designed to sustain an open trading economy, the City of London has benefited enormously from global and national financial de-regulation. Its success has come at a high price, however, if the growth and income prospects of provincial manufacturing regions are taken into account. Whereas the City of London could be thought to occupy the top right-hand cell of the matrix, it is plain that many economic agents located in UK regions more dependent upon labour intensive manufacturing occupy the bottom right-hand cell of the matrix. Whether they are successful or not depends upon their own ability to use existing resources as efficiently and effectively as possible.

Conclusions

Path dependence is a wonderful metaphor. In a simple phrase it manages to capture a variety of common threads of intuition and innovation. With respect to intuition, it represents a methodological and ontological presumption shared by many economic geographers, social theorists and social scientists that the persistence of geographical and historical diversity is systematic. Whereas a great deal of contemporary commentary in mainstream economics is devoted to explaining how and why convergence between economic systems and institutions is accelerating, path dependence represents a way of disputing its proclaimed inevitability. Path dependence is a means of thinking the unthinkable and disputing the convergence to common institutions and functions of economic life (Hollingsworth and Boyer 1997). It is an essential weapon for those who debate the prospects and implications of globalisation. Path dependence is little different, in this context, from other modes and methods of metaphorical thinking in the humanities and social sciences (see generally Lakoff and Johnson 1980; and see Barnes 1994 for geographical examples).

If metaphorical at one level, path dependence has also been a means of analytical and technical innovation. Arthur's (1994) book is both an elaboration of the idea in a quite conventional economic fashion, and an exploration and application of the innovative methods and techniques necessary to sustain the idea in the face of conventional economic techniques designed to prove the existence of singular, optimal landscapes. Whatever his achievements, and however important they have been in underpinning the rapid development of arguments in favour of the persistence of diversity, there remain half hidden from view basic problems with his assumptions about the nature of agent decision-making and behaviour in relation to inherited environments. In this chapter, we have used a rather different metaphor, one owed to Herbert Simon (1956). While recognising the intuitive significance of path dependence, we suggested that its significance is the result of the interaction between agents' cognitive capacities and their place-specific inheritance and endowments.

Our approach is no more conventional than Arthur's. Indeed, it takes aim at the same core assumptions underpinning conventional economic analysis and even the assumptions of the 'new' economic geography (see Clark, Feldman and Gertler 2000). By suggesting that behaviour is contingent, we violate the presumption in favour of the universality of reason, thereby introducing the possibility of persistent heterogeneity across space and time. Furthermore, by using the linked notions of inheritance and endowments we violate the presumption against valuing the past owed to Stanley Jevons (amongst others). Here, the environment is used to represent geographical diversity of relevant institutions, social practices, and local customs and norms. We also suggested that inherited resources can be capitalised into income flows, enabling agents to strategically adapt and respond to European integration and globalisation. Perhaps most provocatively, we have disputed the assumption that regions have the power (or could have the power) of self-determination with respect to the future. We have provided a hierarchy of environments that place regions within national environments (and Europe beyond).

Notice, moreover, that our notion of path dependence provides ample opportunity for economic geographers to add in vital culture-specific ingredients such as language, social practices, and social relationships. Perhaps inevitably, our analysis has been rather schematic and heuristic rather than directly anchored in long-standing cultural practices. So, for example, our analysis could accommodate recent research on relational capital, contextually dependent processes of learning and information processing, and the manner in which expectations are formed by taking advantage of linguistic cues sustained by commonly shared communication practices (Gertler 2002). But this chapter is not a manifesto on behalf of the necessary persistence of diversity. By emphasising the intersection between agents and environments and by providing a means of conceptualising the value of inheritance and endowment in agent decision-making we have also suggested that agents may look outside local circumstances to the economic world beyond. To think otherwise, to imagine that economic agents are always and everywhere local, runs a grave risk of taking the metaphor of path dependence too seriously.

4
Competitive Strategy and Clusters of Innovation

The dominance of large-scale vertically integrated US corporations from around the 1920s onwards, with their elaborate managerial hierarchies and multi-divisional form of organisation, encouraged the belief that smaller craft-based firms were no longer relevant to 'modern' industrial societies because they did not enjoy the economies of scale of larger firms. Schumpeter (1942) played no small part in promoting this belief. He suggested three reasons for assuming a link between firm size and innovation: (1) large firms are in a better position to meet the high costs associated with the design and development of new products and processes; (2) large firms are more likely to have the capacity to absorb the failures and setbacks intrinsic to innovation; and (3) large firms are more able to exert an influence upon the markets in which they compete, and so are better placed to reap the benefits of innovative activity (Teece 1992).[1]

It was not until the last quarter of the 20th century, when the rigidities of large-scale conglomerates, and the success of the so-called information and knowledge economy in regions such as Silicon Valley, became increasingly apparent that economists and other social scientists concerned with economic systems and corporate performance began to take more interest in small firm development. At the same time, there was a dramatic increase in the number of small firms throughout the developed world, and the term 'enterprise culture' came to embody a newfound confidence in their capacity to contribute to economic regeneration (Carter 1996). Our arguments in this chapter are not concerned specifically with small firms, and apply equally to large ones. However, by highlighting the role of small firms (which are generally less well endowed with resources of all kinds than larger ones) in economic development, we are able to draw into focus the capacity of agents to develop strategies to succeed in hugely complex, uncertain and often unforgiving circumstances. Typically, such strategies rely upon networks of interaction involving related firms such as competitors, suppliers and customers. These networks form the focus of this chapter.

The chapter begins by outlining traditional approaches to understanding the environment, and their limitations when the complexity of economic activity and human behaviour are taken into account. Following on from this, we describe the role of networks of interaction in competitive strategy, noting that the relationship between firms and their environments is complex, dynamic and blurred. In the third section of the chapter we consider the importance of network structure, arguing that innovative behavior requires flexibility with regard to network formation. Finally, we discuss the spatial scales at which networks of interaction are most effective. We suggest that clusters of innovation are increasingly international in scope, and that this trend is likely to continue for the foreseeable future.

Competitiveness and the environment

Two (related) aspects of the competitive environment faced by firms across space and across virtually all kinds of economic activity are worth mentioning given their significance in relation to competitiveness. The first is *economic globalisation*. There is a body of opinion which argues that products are increasingly designed and developed in countries which are well-endowed with knowledge and capital, and manufactured in countries where labour costs are low, and that low-tech firms in high-cost regions have become inherently uncompetitive in the face of increased economic integration (Braun and Polt 1988, Arthur 1990). This changing economic geography is seen by many as part of an inevitable and irreversible trend towards post-industrial or knowledge-based societies and economies in the developed world. In the European context, this has led to an obsession with so-called high-tech industries such as pharmaceuticals, biotechnology and aerospace, with low-tech industries often regarded as degrading and indicative of economic weakness. While there is some truth in this analysis, it is an over-simplification that ignores the significant ongoing importance of technically unsophisticated firms in developed economies.[2] Nevertheless, it is hard to ignore the importance of knowledge and learning for competitiveness, and this has led many firms to consider the kinds of strategy required to encourage innovation. Firms have been aided in this respect by developments in communication technologies and transportation which have reduced the transaction costs associated with exporting products, and using subcontractors and/or suppliers in new markets. Increasing harmonisation of regulatory and institutional regimes, especially in the EU, has also reduced the risk and uncertainty associated with cross-border market transactions.

A second issue to be considered is *technological change*, which is both a source and an outcome of competitiveness (Macharzina and Brodel 1996). Firms are being pushed to introduce new products, update existing product lines, and improve production processes and their associated administrative regimes within increasingly short time-frames. Investment in information and process technology is, of course, central to this process: such technology allows for flexibility in manufacturing, enabling firms to customise products without necessarily incurring high costs and to target niche markets. It also allows for the management of information and knowledge, and improved communication with other organisations, including customers and suppliers. However, resource constraints often inhibit firms from investing in many of the technologies that could improve their operational effectiveness. Also, agents may be unaware of some of the options available to them and unsure of the potential benefits they might bring, particularly as the return on investment for a given technology can differ dramatically between industries. A shortage of the skills necessary for the application of such technology presents a further impediment to its acquisition. Shortages of engineers and IT specialists are particularly acute for relatively sophisticated, complex and expensive processes such as computer-aided and computer integrated manufacturing (Panopoulou 2001), and small firms are generally more exposed than large ones in this respect, because they lack the financial resources necessary for recruitment and retention.[3]

The relationship between firms and the competitive environments in which they operate has been a contentious issue in social science. At its core is the extent to which economic agents are able to manage issues such as globalisation and technological change in order to create the conditions for their future success. Much of the analysis has taken a deterministic perspective, assuming that behaviour is governed by, and essentially a reaction to, structural constraints. In other words, agents simply respond to their environments, with little or no capacity for strategic choice. A number of different strands to this body of work can be identified drawing upon Whittington (1988), Child (1996), and our discussion in Chapter 2.

Action determinism is rooted in a conception of human behaviour as super-rational, maximising and optimising: agents are driven by a desire to maximise returns from any given level of spending, and firms by a desire to maximise production from any given level of input. The aggregate of individual maximisation is an economic system that ensures the efficient allocation of resources in general and capital in particular. The implication, presumably, is that agents have almost unlimited cognitive capacities and are not restricted by time or by shortages of knowledge and information (Gigerenzer 2001). Also absent are notions of power, ideology and emotion, or indeed any social process which might influence behaviour. Although it is an approach which derives from 19th century neo-classical economics and classical management theory, it remains an influential reference point for many social scientists, albeit packaged in a more sophisticated way. Thus Michael Jensen (1998, 40), for example, argues that 'it is inconceivable that purposeful action on the part of human beings can be viewed as anything other than responses to incentives. Indeed, the issue of incentives goes to the heart of what it means to maximise or optimise, in fact to the very core of what it means to choose. Rational individuals always choose the option that makes them better off as they see it. This is, by definition, what we mean by purposeful action – the attempt to accomplish some end'. These apparently simple agents act in entirely predictable ways to environmental stimuli, and are essentially removed from the contexts in which they operate; the behaviour of agents is determined by overbearing psychological mechanisms that effectively bypass conscious decision-making (Whittington 1988).

Environmental determinism does not make assumptions regarding the cognitive capacities of agents. Rather, it assumes that organisations are governed by their situations. Successful organisations are those that best fit, or adapt to, the contexts in which they operate. Organisational ecology focuses specifically on how firms in a given industry exploit resource opportunities in a given market, and the ways in which the environment favours or 'selects' particular strategies (Zammuto 1988). Material determinants such as the number of persons in an organisation, the scope of the products or services offered, and the prevailing market conditions constrain agents to such an extent that only a very limited number of strategies allow for firm survival (Aldrich 1979, Hannan and Freeman 1989, Gambarotto and Maggioni 1998). This approach denies that intended action contributes to social and economic change (Giddens 1986). Proponents do not deny purposeful behaviour, but regard it as irrelevant for understanding social systems: 'No matter what men's motives are, the outcome is determined not by the individual participants, but by an environment beyond their control' (Penrose 1952, 808–9). Thus, although agents can theoretically exercise choice and free will, in reality the range of options available to them is severely limited by contextual factors. Although environmental determinism has become unfashionable in much of social science, it is a concept that continues to appear in other guises.[4]

A more sophisticated, and in many ways more powerful, approach to understanding agents and environments is the *new institutional economics*. Although this is a 'broad church' that contains a number of competing positions, fundamental to this approach is the claim that institutions provide the strategic context for agents' behaviour (Steinmo and Tolbert 1998). The structural forms of institutions, it is argued, as well as the identities and values that sustain them, 'map themselves' onto firms which rely on them for their existence (Child 1996). Firms and other organisations are considered as social phenomena whose objectives and practices are moulded by the complex networks of beliefs, value systems and conventions in which they are embedded. Crucially, this environment is considered to be objectively rather than subjectively determined. Although the structure and behaviour of firms is explained by reference to the 'taken-for-granted scripts of organisational reality' (Beckert 1999), rather than maximising or optimising strategies, the implications of the institutional approach are all too clear: agency and strategic choice do not form central components of the decision-making process.

Economic behaviour, alliances and competitive strategy

In each of the three models outlined in the previous section, organisational characteristics and behaviour are assumed to be products of the contexts in which they operate. In the first two approaches, agents are removed from the social world, and from the formal and informal customs and norms that sustain behaviour. In all three cases, societies and economies are assumed to be homogenous and objectively determined, with their constituent members sharing belief and value systems that dictate their behaviour in response to incentives.

They also assume a static view of culture, and struggle to explain why social systems change over time except by reference to purely economic phenomena. Figure 4.1 illustrates the conventional view of agent-environment interaction in economics and business strategy. It is a way of viewing the world which has been influenced by the three approaches outlined above and which contains assumptions gleaned from them: (1) firms and their environments are sepa-

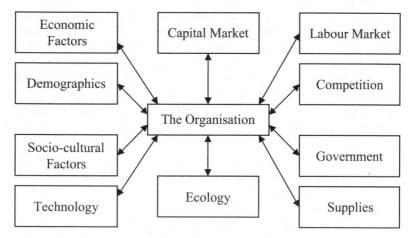

Figure 4.1   A conventional approach to agent-environment interaction
Source: Van Witteloostuijin (1996: 756)

rate entities with clearly defined boundaries; (2) firms have no control of their environments and which aspects of them are relevant; (3) firms must adapt to environmental conditions in order to be successful; and (4) adaptive behaviour is facilitated by the maximising and optimising behaviour of individuals and their firms.

As economic geographers, sociologists and management theorists have built up a clearer picture of the nature of the innovation process, and decision making more generally, the shortcomings of this approach have become increasingly apparent. (Cf. Burt 1992, Child 1972, 1997, Sewell 1992, Teece 1992, and White 2002). The relationship between firms and their environments is complex, dynamic and blurred, and the two cannot be considered as discrete. Firms are, of course, located within complex economic, political and social systems that encourage some kinds of action and limit others. However, as Child (1997) articulates clearly, agent-environment interaction is a two-way process in which agents may have the capacity to manipulate their environments for their own purposes, just as the behaviour of agents influences their context. Firms regularly interact and build alliances with organisations that form part of their environments (such as suppliers, customers, competitors etc.) over which they are sometimes able to impose a degree of control that is deemed legitimate by both parties, and in this respect agents rely heavily on their capacity to persuade, coerce, accommodate, and collaborate with other actors. Thus the nature of some aspects of firms' environments may be negotiated through networks of social interaction between agents and their counterparts in other relevant organisations. This obviates the need to look for clearly defined boundaries to firms.[5] In many ways the contemporary economic environment might be described as *alliance capitalism*. Alliances may involve a variety of different partners. They can occur between functional departments and/or subsidiaries within the same firm, between firms and their competitors,[6] between complementary firms such as suppliers, customers, subcontractors and distributors, between private firms and public institutions such as universities and regional and national governments, between different kinds of public institution, or between firms and other stakeholders and interest groups which operate within market-based systems of accumulation such as consumers, trades unions and environmentalists (Dunning 1999). In practice, networks of interaction often involve a combination of two or more of the above alliances. Alliances also vary in terms of their formality and their governance structures. Increasingly, however, it appears that they are informal rather than contractual. In other words, in place of formal relationships between actors which are internalised in hierarchies and thus at least partly sheltered from market forces, many firms are choosing to engage in alliances with external organisations which tend to rely upon trust rather than legal processes for their governance (Dunning 1999, Ozawa 1999). As Teece (1992) pointed out, this is often overlooked by scholars obsessed by the minutiae of property rights and legal titles. Hotz-Hart (2000, 434) neatly summarised the potential benefits of networks of interaction:

1. *Better access to information, knowledge, skills and experience.* In particular, networks provide opportunities for learning about new ways of operating and about new forms of technology, and can reduce the development time and cost of new products and production processes.
2. *Improved linkages and cooperation between network members*, particularly between users and suppliers. The competence of the leading firms within a network can form a benchmark for others. Effective networks can encourage interactive learning, synergy and complementarity between key specialist groups across participating firms, such as design, production, marketing and finance.
3. *Improved response capacity.* Networks allow participating firms to respond more quickly and to anticipate changing competitive circumstances, and to learn about new forms of technology.
4. *Reduced risk, moral hazards, information and transaction costs.* Networks of firms with complementary assets allow resources to be shared and reduce costs. Risks can also be assessed and shared throughout the network leading to more informed decisions and further cost reductions.
5. *Improved trust and social cohesion.* Alliances encourage shared values, goals, norms and ways of working which facilitate problem-solving, collective action and innovative behaviour, often through a complex combination of competition and cooperation.

Networks of interaction have assumed particular significance in recent years because of their presumed importance for learning and innovation. These concepts will not be discussed in detail here, as they are the focus of Chapter 5. At this juncture it is sufficient to point out that networks are thought to encourage interactive learning between participating organisations through the sharing of knowledge and information, which is itself facilitated through trust, shared values and ways of working. Ultimately, the aim is the development of new products and processes, but it may also include the exploitation of new technology, the introduction of new skills, and/or the development of new markets. The vast body of literature that has emerged is, however, incredibly fragmented, encompassing an array of theoretical positions and perspectives. In this chapter we focus upon two issues which we believe to be of particular significance and which need clarification in order to move to a clearer understanding of the ways in which networks of interaction evolve, and of their capabilities and limitations in relation to economic performance and competitiveness: (1) the importance of network structure, arguing that innovative activity requires flexibility with regard to network formation. (2) The role of geography in relation to the formation and functioning of networks. It is our contention that networks are likely to be increasingly international in scope.

Network structure and innovation

A landmark paper that continues to form a crucial reference point for social scientists interested in the role of networks in social and economic life is Granovetter's (1973) essay on the 'strength of weak ties'. The argument he sets out stems from his empirical work on careers in which he challenged neo-classical analyses of labour markets on the grounds of what he believed were the unrealistic assumptions they made about human behaviour and social structure. He conducted a study in which he sought to understand how individuals came to be employed in their current positions. He noted that when his respondents found employment via a personal contact such contacts were generally distant, perhaps a chance encounter with a former colleague, rather than through well established familial relationships or friendships. These more distant contacts were particularly useful because they provided access to new flows of information and permitted action which was not constrained by group loyalties or expectations. He concluded that 'weak ties, often denounced as generative of alienation... are seen here as indispensable to individuals' opportunities and to their integration into communities; strong ties, breeding local cohesion, lead to overall fragmentation' (p. 1378). Building explicitly on the work of Granovetter, Burt (1992) used the term 'structural holes' to describe the bridge between firms or groups of firms which are not otherwise connected.

These ideas have been developed by scholars interested in issues such as innovation, entrepreneurship and competitiveness. (See, for example, Grabher 1993; Sabel 1995). The argument is essentially very simple: weak ties provide a link to other firms and networks with different ways of viewing the world, and are therefore important for the introduction of new ideas and perspectives. These ties act as bridges across which alternate information flows can travel and are crucial for innovative behaviour. By way of contrast, strong, well established networks are effective at transmitting information between participating firms, but tend to be poor sources of new ideas and ways of working. This propensity increases over time – as firms learn more about one another, they come to view situations from increasingly similar perspectives.

Other scholars work on the assumption that close, strong ties between firms are required for innovation and competitiveness. This is most obvious in the literature on spatial clustering, but in strategic management strong ties between related firms also tend to be a fundamental reference point. Much of the reasoning stems from the view that trust and learning within networks are crucial for innovation and successful relationships, and that strong links between firms are necessary for these to be achieved. Child and Faulkner (1998), for example, noted that 'bonding' was a 'significant requirement for alliance success' (p. 56) and that network partnerships were more likely to 'evolve progressively' if participating firms committed themselves to mutual learning for an indefinite period. In a similar vein, Perry (1996) noted that 'Network relations depend on long-term personal association from which trust and reciprocal relations emerge' (p. 77), while Teece (2000) argued that central players with strong links to suppliers and customers are better able both to drive and to benefit from innovative activities. Teece has also argued convincingly that innovations which demand the development of new technological systems or platforms to support them require close integration of people and knowledge from many organisations, as a single company (regardless of its size) is unlikely to contain the range of knowledge and expertise necessary for this type of innovation.[1]

From these two perspectives (weak versus strong ties) it seems that two prototypical approaches to innovation can be inferred. These are illustrated in Figures 4.2 and 4.3. In the case of weak ties (Figure 4.2), proponents envisage a process whereby firms or groups of firms source ideas and opportunities from other firms or networks with which they have only rudimentary relationships. These links may become closer should the relevant parties decide to collaborate on the development of a specific product or technology as illustrated by path 1, or may involve the simple exchange of knowledge

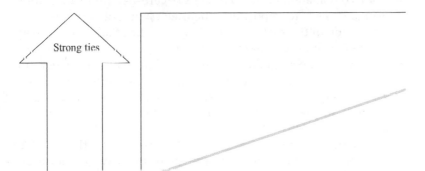

Figure 4.2   Weak ties and innovation

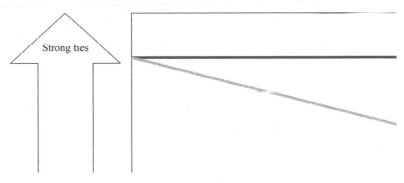

Figure 4.3   Strong ties and innovation

and information, with ties remaining distant as illustrated by path 2. In the case of strong ties (Figure 4.3), on the other hand, innovation is deemed to derive from the close interaction between members of a particular network where shared values and ways of working facilitate problem solving and decision-making. The maintenance of strong ties is likely to be necessary for much of the life cycle of the product or technology as illustrated by path 3, although it may be that strong ties are required principally for the identification of opportunities, and will become weaker over time as illustrated by path 4.

Both of these approaches underestimate the complexity of the networks in which firms are situated: innovative firms rely on a dynamic combination of strong and weak ties. At any one time, innovative firms will be involved in multiple relationships that follow a combination of the four paths (Figure 4.4). Innovative firms continually seek to reposition themselves in order to find the configuration of ties that is most suitable for the attainment of their objectives, given the contexts in which they operate. It stands to reason that each configuration of ties is unique and that there is no 'best' network arrangement. However, firms characterised only by weak or strong ties, or by hardly any ties at all, are much less likely to achieve strong market positions regardless of the industry in which they compete.

In practice, an important factor in determining the relative balance of strong and weak ties is likely to be the pace of innovation

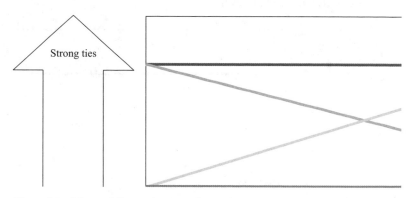

Figure 4.4   Network formation as a dynamic process

in a given market (dramatic versus continuous but limited improvements to products and production processes). Networks characterised mainly by strong ties are likely to promote more direct monitoring and control, improved problem solving capacity, increased stability in decision making and increased commitment to other stakeholders. But, as noted below, this commitment to particular policies and/or groups may also make companies resistant to technical, market and other external changes. In addition to access to new ideas and ways of working, the advantage of weaker ties is that control is less concentrated and it may therefore be easier to adapt to external factors. Thus each configuration is probably better suited to particular sectors. Industries in which there is a degree of uncertainty and rapid technical change, such as software development, electronics and pharmaceuticals, may be better suited to weaker ties. Sectors that are more reliant on established markets and where technical development is more gradual, such as mechanical engineering and vehicles, may be better suited to more stable network structures.

Even within these broad archetypes, however, there will be considerable diversity over time as new opportunities emerge and circumstances alter (see, for example, Lazerson and Lorenzoni 1999). Clusters of firms linked by strong ties are not necessarily enduring, and necessarily evolve during the lifecycle of a particular product, market or technology. Even core firms which appear to be most 'embedded' in a particular network, may become peripheral and look to other networks over time should they consider that their interests could be served better elsewhere, or should other firms consider their membership of little value (or indeed counterproductive). Likewise, peripheral firms with weak ties to a particular cluster may develop stronger ties over time and become part of the core group, bringing with them their own sets of ties and links to which other participating firms are exposed. The key point is that *flexibility* in terms of the construction and reformulation of appropriate network forms constitutes a crucial component of competitiveness.

However, the difficulty is that there are powerful forces which mediate against flexibility of network formation and the flow of information between firms: individuals (and their firms) tend to find change uncomfortable and disorientating and may develop defensive routines that protect their roles and current ways of working (Argyris and Schön 1996). This is compounded by the fact that the social world embraces a number of assumptions which tend not be questioned by agents. Taken for granted norms and ways of thinking impose artificial restrictions on decision-making and behaviour both within and between firms which are often sustained and reinforced through observation of others' behaviour, social interaction and consensus building (Morgan 1997, Weick 1979). Where flexibility is absent within networks, and where the roles and behaviour of participating firms become routinised and taken for granted, the formulation of strategy may be seriously impaired. Under these circumstances, agents can, and often do, become prisoners of their environments by making decisions within fixed frames of reference which effectively take the form of negative feedback loops, reinforcing existing patterns of behaviour. Such behaviour is often termed single-loop learning. This is embodied most obviously in standard operating procedures that articulate expected behaviour for specific situations, with little latitude for the introduction of new ideas. Janis (1982) used the term 'groupthink' to describe decision-making processes that prioritise group cohesiveness rather than the development of effective solutions, the consequence of which is an absence of critical thinking. In a similar vein, Bathelt (2001) used the work of Kern (1996) to illustrate the danger of 'blind confidence, gullibility and lock-in' (p. 5) within networks of interaction. Where actors are convinced of the effectiveness of their network's operating procedures and strategies for problem solving, agents may continue to rely upon them well beyond the point at which they have been rendered redundant.

The functioning of networks may be further constrained by political factors (Morgan 1997). Networks (and their constituent organisations) contain a number of individuals, interest groups and coalitions that often come into conflict with one another and whose ambitions may or may not coincide with the 'best' interests of the network as a whole. Conflict may manifest itself through the manipulation of information, through hostility and a lack of trust between participating organisations (or individuals and groups within them), and through an unwillingness to cooperate with partners. This may be exacerbated by specialisation and departmentalisation within and between firms that create sub-units with separate goals and tasks. Often, these sub-units develop their own commitments and outlooks based on values, attitudes and beliefs that are self-reinforcing. The decision-making process thus involves negotiation or bargaining between interest groups with different levels of influence. In this way, decisions are rarely taken simply, but instead emerge from interaction between individuals, organisations and contextual factors. Thus firms and networks of firms can be considered to be political systems that contain many competing or overlapping rationalities. It could be argued that power differentials within networks of firms can facilitate decision-making and help to resolve disputes. However, more extreme power differentials within networks may lead to expediency and unscrupulous behaviour (Bathelt 2002, Granovetter 1985).

Despite the existence of powerful organisational defence mechanisms and political activity within and between firms that are intended to resist change, agents do have the capacity to question more fundamental aspects of firms' environments, including taken for granted norms and behaviour (often called double- and triple-loop learning). Indeed the ability to conceptualise the social world from different perspectives and to challenge prevailing operating norms and assumptions is crucial if agents are to influence their environments in meaningful ways. In addition to organisational assumptions and norms, double- and triple-loop learning require agents to understand the frameworks, paradigms, metaphors, mindsets and mental models that underpin relationships within and between firms, and to challenge and alter them, as well as develop alternative ones, at appropriate junctures (Morgan 1997). The work of Peter Senge (1992) is relevant here. He argues that agents need to restructure how they think about organisational reality. This involves 'a shift of mind from seeing parts to seeing wholes, from seeing people as helpless reactors to seeing them as active participants in shaping their reality, from reacting to the present to creating the future' (p. 69). To learn in this way, existing patterns of decision-making must be deconstructed, reframed, and altered accordingly. This continual shifting, breaking down and creation of paradigms is central to our conception of agency, and crucial to meaningful cooperation between firms (see Chapter 6). For firms, at issue is how best to construct alliances and participate in networks which encourage this type of behaviour.

Regional clusters of innovation

We can draw three lessons from the previous discussion which are relevant to our understanding of regional development and how it might be re-conceptualised. (1) flexibility in terms of network formation is crucial for problem solving, innovation and competitiveness; (2) networks contain powerful forces which inhibit flexibility, encouraging conformity and increasing the likelihood of market failure; and (3) firms and the networks of which they are part have the capacity to overcome these barriers and 'learn how to learn' on a collective basis. These points have important implications for the spatial forms and dynamics of contemporary capitalism.

Most analyses of agglomeration emphasise the importance of geographical proximity for promoting and sustaining the kinds of relationship necessary for innovation. For Storper (1997), this is because 'untraded interdependencies' such as trust, shared norms and structures, and familiar values are more likely to exist between firms located in the same jurisdiction, while Lundvall (1992), Feldman (1994) and Malmberg (1997) stressed the importance of shared institutional and cultural contexts for encouraging interactive learning between actors. These ideas are, of course, far from new, and can be traced at least as far back as Marshall's (1890) commentary on industrial districts. Increasingly, scholars point to what they see as the context bound, firm-specific and tacit nature of knowledge, arguing that these form significant barriers to its articulation and transferral (Polanyi 1966, Nelson and Winter 1982, Lam 1997). This kind of knowledge is termed 'sticky' because it is embedded in social relations and team dynamics, and cannot be easily formalised. Rather, intense social interaction is thought to be crucial to the transfer of knowledge and to the development of 'communities of knowing' (Boland and Tenkasi 1995).

To the extent that economic globalisation is accepted as a reality in these analyses, it is thought to reinforce, rather than dilute, local specialisation. By this logic, increasing numbers of firms and regions around the world will tend towards local specialisation as a means of improving their market positions in the face of global competition. Because proximity is assumed to be a prerequisite for agglomeration and to form a significant barrier to the formation of close ties, it is assumed that these clusters will remain essentially regional in character, connected only loosely and with limited inter-regional collaboration. Storper (2000), for example, argued that globalisation is (or at least thus far has been) 'soft' in nature, principally taking the form of trade in goods and the exchange of ideas, with little change in output and locational specialisation. Beyond this, there is little discussion of how sophisticated networks of interaction dispersed across space might contribute to innovation and improved problem solving.

It is our view that this position exaggerates the importance of tacit knowledge and face-to-face interaction for innovation and competitiveness. (see Chapter 6). To retreat into arguments about the cultural nature of knowledge and the importance of shared values represents a form of cultural and intellectual imperialism which ignores the demonstrated ability of human beings to understand the social world of which they are a part, and to build bridges that allow for mutual understanding. By emphasising geography rather than the thought and action of agents in economic development, this view risks unwittingly reinforcing the deterministic paradigm in social science. It also illustrates the tendency of social scientists to deny economic agents the very capacities that they take for granted in the course of their analyses of social and economic life. Perhaps most importantly, it ignores the real dangers of homogeneity in relation to innovation and the real benefits that can accrue from heterogeneity in this respect.

Networks of interaction will increasingly be international in scope as firms seek to find partners with the best 'fit' in relation to the kinds of products they develop and the markets in which they compete, regardless of geography. This does not imply that the ties between the firms will necessarily be weaker; we believe that the kind of dynamic that presently exists and that is so admired in regions such as Silicon Valley and Route 128 can be developed further on an international basis. Indeed, the diversity of perspectives that would result from these arrangements may present a crucial source of competitive advantage. Our arguments have particular relevance for Europe where firms are often forced by the relatively small size of their domestic markets to look outside national borders for potential partners and customers. In the case of the US, firms are more likely to look in the first instance to other American regions. But even so, the competitiveness of US firms would surely be constrained were they to restrict their search for partners within their national boundaries.

Many economists and geographers have tended to ignore a large body of work, both theoretical and empirical, by scholars specialising in international and cross-cultural management (see, for example, Hall 1995 and Trompenaars 1997) as well as an older body of work by social psychologists on decision-making and problem solving (see, for example, Hoffman and Maier 1961, and Triandis, Hall and Ewan 1965). In addition to the difficulties often encountered when managing across cultures, what emerges from this literature is how flexible and innovative actors can be at building bridging mechanisms which promote mutual understanding, and the advantages of diversity for creativity and problem-solving. In an insightful study, Moss Kanter and Corn (1994) examined eight foreign acquisitions of US companies in order to look for situations in which cross-cultural interaction might cause friction between the respective parties. They found cultural differences to be relatively unimportant as sources of tension: organisational and/or technical considerations were deemed far more significant for the success or failure of a given merger. Cultural heterogeneity was shown to be overstated, and an easy excuse which employees (and researchers) latched onto in order to explain tensions whose actual causes were far more deep-rooted.[8]

Other factors also lead us to believe that networks may disperse further. For instance, new kinds of communication technologies and advanced transportation have allowed for the rapid formation and reorganisation of local and global linkages and networks. While we accept Storper's (2000) point that the ideas put forward by Castells (1996) and other theorists of the 'information age' are inadequate because they consider information as 'disembodied bits of knowledge in relation to hardware' (p. 152), it is nevertheless true that advances in communication technology have facilitated the development of interactive forms of knowledge creation across space and allowed production units the flexibility to adjust their corporate strategies and organisational forms quickly in response to technological and market fluctuations (Ernst 2001). Also, production units increasingly source technological and other knowledge from outside the industrial district in which they are based in order to gain access to specialist labour markets and other location-specific resources. Consequently geographical clusters can no longer be (if, indeed, they ever could be) thought of simply as closed local systems. In this respect, the growing power of transnational corporations (TNCs) in production networks must be acknowledged Dicken (1992), for example, noted that 'TNCs operate within intricate networks of externalised relationships... [which] add to the kaleidoscopic complexity of the global economy... Both internalised and externalised relationships are the threads through which the global economy is integrated, linking together both organisations and geographical areas in complex, interrelated and overlapping divisions of labour' (p. 226). See also Taylor and Thrift (1982).

By making these points we do not seek to deny the central importance of regional systems of innovation for economic development. In order to compete in a global environment firms may have to strengthen their participation within regional networks which are themselves likely to increase in importance. We also accept, as was discussed in Chapter 3, that the market position of firms is profoundly affected by their inherited local resources and institutions. Some communities are characterised by high levels of inherited formal and informal institutional support (social and relational capital) that strengthen competitiveness. Other regions are less expedient. Although agents may choose to select, adapt or ignore aspects of their inheritance, this depends upon the availability of economic resources as well as information and knowledge about prospective opportunities. In some circumstances, therefore, inherited institutions and resources form significant barriers that severely restrict the development potential of firms, and perhaps even of the regions in which they are based. In other circumstances inherited resources and institutions can reinforce existing virtuous patterns of growth: firms can use their strong positions to generate more easily the conditions for their future success. It is important to note that firms situated in jurisdictions with high levels of social capital which manifests itself in, say, productive relationships between manufacturers and suppliers is no guarantee of participation in effective networks. Firms must work hard to build relationships and mutual understanding within and outside the regions in which they are based.

Nor would we go as far to suggest that these trends (and the resulting sharing of knowledge and information) necessarily result in economic convergence, as is often assumed in economics and geography.[9] As Storper (2000) and many other economic geographers have demonstrated, the situation is considerably more complex than this idealised picture. Although the exchange of knowledge and information does encourage convergence by allowing local production systems to achieve international standards of best practice, the nature and speed of technical development and knowledge diffusion vary significantly between economies. Because these are important determinants of economic performance, spatial inequalities may be exaggerated as well as reduced. Also, superior transportation and communication networks and the existence of specialist labour markets may reinforce in a cumulative manner the competitiveness of currently successful regions, forming a significant barrier to convergence (Amin and Tomaney 1995, Dunford and Perrons 1994).

Conclusions

More than forty years ago Herbert Simon (1956) argued that the analysis of human behaviour must take into account the cognitive limits of economic agents and the structure of the environments in which they operate, as well as the fact that agents are able to exploit these structures in order to achieve their objectives. In this chapter we have built upon these insights by exploring the ways that economic agents collaborate with other actors in order to improve their market positions. This does not imply that we idealise agent capacity. We do not wish to suggest that firms have the potential to create unlimited opportunities or to overcome market conditions of any sort through participation in such networks. There are limits to agent capacity and to what can be achieved through collaboration. Indeed, we have noted that networks of interaction may constrain the competitiveness of firms in some circumstances. However, we have been careful to avoid using the term 'embedded' (Granovetter 1985) to describe the position of firms within networks of interaction. To us, this implies that firms are passive in terms of their choice of collaborators and patterns of behaviour.

In practice, firms increasingly demonstrate the capacity to build relationships through new and innovative forms of organisation (Grabher 2001 and Teece 2000). For Europe in particular, these ties are increasingly international in scope as firms located in relatively small jurisdictions seek the most appropriate partners, regardless of their geography, in order to improve their competitive positions. In this respect we believe that agents can, and increasingly are, overcoming the barriers of culture and distance. The relative significance of regional, national and international networks does, of course, vary between industries and is likely to depend at least partly on the transaction, production and coordination costs of decentralisation (Dunning 1998, Scott 1998). Nevertheless, there are reasons to suppose that while clusters may be localised entities such as regions, they may also constitute spatially elongated networks across higher spatial scales, and that this is likely to be increasingly common by virtue of the benefits of advanced transportation and communication systems.

While much has been written about the form and benefits of networks of interaction, economists and geographers have shown little interest in the *nature* of the interaction itself, relying instead upon institutions (vaguely defined) as mechanisms which regulate behaviour. In the following chapter we address this lacuna by taking cognition and patterns of thought seriously as determinants of economic performance, whilst acknowledging the role of institutions and systems of management and organisation. Using the information and knowledge economy to illustrate our argument, we assume that the development of firms, industries and regions is linked to the thought and action of the agents that create and sustain them.

5
Cognition, Learning and the New Economy

Since the early 1980s, the economic performance of continental EU economies has been generally modest. Whether measured by rates of unemployment, rates of employment growth or economic growth, Europe has consistently under-performed compared to its immediate Atlantic competitor. Although the reasons for their contrasting fortunes are complex and multi-faceted, the emergence of the so-called information and knowledge economy in the US and its limited development in much of the EU appears to have been an important factor. At the Lisbon summit of European leaders in March 2000, the need for greater dynamism and entrepreneurship within Europe was widely noted. Delegates focused on the 'paradigm shift driven by globalisation and the new knowledge economy' and recognised that a 'radical transformation of Europe's economy and society' is needed if it is to keep pace with the US. With the likely accession of a number of near-neighbours from central and eastern Europe to the EU, these issues are ever more important for the future development and social cohesion of Europe. European policy makers take these concerns seriously; unless the EU improves its competitive position, it will be unable to sustain its social and political objectives.

The development of the information and knowledge economy and the increasing importance of the global economy suggest that we are moving into a new phase of economic development. According to Teece (2000), the growth of the information and knowledge economy can be explained by reference to characteristics such as the rapid and cost-effective exchange of information, the

91

expansion of markets for different types of products, the deregulation of product and labour markets, and the increased flow of financial assets around the world. At its core, however, is 'the development and astute deployment and utilisation of intangible assets of which knowledge, competence, and intellectual property are the most significant' (p. 3). Furthermore, the knowledge economy is believed to have a distinctive geography – regional clusters of innovation, technology, and human and social capital, as illustrated by Silicon Valley, Rt 128/495 Boston, and (in the UK) Cambridgeshire and Oxfordshire (Lawton Smith 2001). This point was also made by Antonelli (2001) who noted that 'the regional and technological concentration of innovation activities' suggests the growing importance of endogenous forces of growth (set against conventional expectations that export-led growth is the model for all nations).

For some, new kinds of knowledge have replaced the long-established sources of competitive advantage that dominated mainstream economic thought since the publication of Adam Smith's (1776) *The Wealth of Nations*: endowments of natural resources, concentrations of capital, the availability of labour, and economies of scale. See, for example, Blackler (1995). The veracity of these claims is not entirely clear; knowledge was, of course, central to virtually all kinds of economic activity long before the notion of the information and knowledge economy entered social scientific discourse, and most work has always relied upon intuitive, tacit and unarticulated stores of knowledge (Ackroyd, Glover, Currie and Bull 2000). In our view, the significance of the information and knowledge cannot be adequately understood just in terms of the importance or otherwise of knowledge *per se*, or because it appears to be a distinctive geographical form, or because the industries normally associated with it rely upon forms of knowledge that are fundamentally different or more esoteric from that of other industries.[1] The essence of the information and knowledge economy, and what makes it a very real phenomenon which has profoundly affected rates of labour productivity, innovation and economic growth, are the distinctive ways in which knowledge is created and disseminated between constituent actors, and the accompanying changes to the organisation of firms, industries and regions.

Recent years have seen terms such as 'the learning region' and 'the learning organisation' become important in the lexicon of social scientists concerned about competitiveness and competitive advantage. In many respects these concepts form the basis of our understanding of the information and knowledge economy, although their use is by no means confined to the study of knowledge-based industries. Instinctively, we are uncomfortable with this terminology. We begin with the assumption that cognitive capacity is the domain of human beings; organisations and regions do not possess consciousness. Nevertheless, we also assume that agents cannot be considered without taking into account the contexts in which they operate. Firms, regions and their associated institutions are crucial for individual and collective learning and for innovative behaviour in general. Specifically, they provide structural and procedural mechanisms and channels of communication that enable the collation, manipulation, analysis, and dissemination of knowledge and information. More importantly, through the use of routines and conventions, we believe that organisations and regions can institutionalise ways of thinking, thereby exerting a powerful influence on behaviour (Levitt and March 1988) Any theory of learning and innovation must be able to accommodate the interaction between individual, group, organisational and regional or societal levels of action that this implies. However, despite the endurance and persistence of many institutions and decision-making routines, we do not believe that they have an existence independent of the actors who sustain them, or that they necessarily overwhelm individual consciousness so that agents are oblivious to their existence. We consider agent-environment interaction to be a two-way process, one in which agents may have the capacity to manipulate their environments for their own purposes just as their surroundings may directly affect agent behaviour. (See Chapters 2 and 3.)

The next section of the chapter outlines our views about the nature of cognition, a subject which has been much-neglected within economics and geography but one which we believe to be crucial for understanding innovation and economic development. In the third section we outline a tripartite conception of learning based on the work of Argyris and Schön (1978, 1996) and which forms the theoretical basis for our arguments. This is followed by our model of innovation with respect to the information and knowledge economy which seeks to describe and explain the complex interactions between the relevant cognitive, institutional and organisational factors. In the penultimate section our model is discussed in the context of European regional development. In doing so we are mindful that Europe is a very different economic environment to the US. Finally we discuss the prospects for, and limits to, knowledge-based activity in Europe.

The nature of cognition

The capacity to think and learn is surely a most remarkable characteristic of human beings, and as such it has long been a focus of study for social scientists. The doctrine of rationality has formed a central component of this body of knowledge. Indeed, it has underpinned much social scientific thought related to the nature of the self, society and culture since Spinoza (1632–77) and Leibnitz (1646–1716) (Sedgwick 1999). At the beginning of the 21st century, its influence remains strongest in economics, where the view of agents as rational, utility maximising subjects continues to dominate the mainstream of the subject (Hodgson 1996). According to the theory of subjective utility (SEU theory), decision-making comprises three basic elements (Simon 1987): (1) choices are made among a fixed set of alternatives all of which are known to agents; (2) agents are aware of the probability distributions with regard to the outcome of each option; and (3) choices reflect agents' desire to maximise the expected value of a given utility function. This approach, rooted in positivism and scientism, assumes that learning occurs experientially through trial and error and that knowledge consists of accumulated discrete events each of which are observable. The systematic nature of behaviour implies that patterns of knowledge can be discerned and measured. Proponents of this approach argue that it is possible to measure and explain behaviour with a view to making empirical generalisations.

Previously, we used Simon's (1956, 1997) notion of 'bounded rationality' as the basis of our objections to the rational paradigm, and Simon's work remains a powerful reference point for understanding cognition and decision-making (Tracey, Clark and Lawton Smith 2001). By his logic, the ability of individuals, groups or firms to behave in rational ways is constrained by (1) limited resources, interests, knowledge; (2) limited cognitive capacity; and (3) the environment in which they operate. Decision-makers do not have all of the relevant information available, nor do they have the cognitive capacity to process such information in the needed SEU 'scientific' fashion. Because agents make decisions knowing only some of the likely consequences of their actions, they 'satisfice' rather than optimise or maximise; they choose an option which they believe will at least meet *a priori* specified criteria. This is true of apparently straightforward decisions, but is especially the case in decisions which have a strategic dimension: the more important the decision to be made, the greater the number of factors to be considered, and the more far-reaching (but ill-defined) the consequences (Clark and Marshall 2002).[2]

Whilst acknowledging the limitations of the human mind, in other ways the bounded rationality model assumes that agents' behaviour is more sophisticated than the rational paradigm implies. This is perhaps most evident when agents deal with situations where outcomes and goals are incommensurable. In circumstances where decisions are likely to result in both positive and negative consequences, or where different interest groups are likely to be affected in different ways, no optimal choice can be made. The complexity of all but the most basic problems means that agents rely heavily on *heuristics*, or rules of thumb, for making inferences and ultimately decisions about their worlds. Heuristics are perhaps best described as the generic application of rules to situations subject to the limitations of time, knowledge and cognitive capacity; they are particularly important when the range of available options is unclear, and where information about the options themselves (and their likely outcomes) is limited (Gigerenzer and Todd 1999). Considered in this way, heuristics are essentially strategies to simplify, systemise and economise on decision-making.

Although the heuristics employed differ between cognitive tasks and adaptive problems (adaptive problems tend to use emotions rather than cognitive mechanisms to aid decision making), they each share three common building blocks: they search, they stop search and they make a decision. Searching involves the investigation of (1) alternatives (the choice set) and (2) cues (for evaluating the alternatives). Common search schemas include random search, ordered search (for example, considering cues in relation to their validities), and search imitation (which allows humans to learn quickly from others of where to look and what to look for). For adaptive tasks, emotions such as fear and disgust can narrow choice sets dramatically. According to Simon (1955), the search process is stopped when a course of action is found which matches or exceeds the aspiration level (this is the essence of his 'satisficing' concept). For Gigerenzer, however, several (possibly competing) goals with different aspiration levels are likely to co-exist in any given situation and so search stops 'as soon as the first cue that favors one alternative is found' (2001, 44). A decision or inference is made when the search process has ended. When making important or strategic decisions, agents endeavour to weigh up the consequences of particular alternatives. For less significant decisions, however, the difficulties inherent in this task means that attempts to weight alternative factors or to develop a common currency to facilitate comparison are limited.

Agents do not, of course, exist in isolation. The organisational, social and geographical contexts in which they operate provide powerful cues for behaviour in the form of norms and customs, which are themselves underpinned by shared beliefs and meaning. The heuristics that agents develop to make inferences about their worlds are often transposed onto the structures and modes of operation of organisations and other institutions that comprise their environment. These institutional heuristics help to further divide, routinise and bind together the decision-making process in order to make it manageable. As Morgan (1997) points out, divisions of labour serve not only to facilitate the allocation of human and other resources but also create 'a structure of attention, information, interpretation, and decision-making that exerts a crucial influence on an organisation's daily operation' (p. 79). This allows agents to 'take advantage of the structure of the information in the environment to arrive at meaningful decisions' (Gigerenzer and Todd 1999, 28). In other words, agents rely on institutions, at varying levels of aggregation, as mechanisms to assist decision-making and in order to 'enact' their environments.

A model of learning

In explaining learning and innovation in the information and knowledge economy, many scholars in geography and in economics have moved away from models of SEU rationality, arguing that economic activity is a socially embedded process that takes place within institutional and cultural frameworks (Grabher 1993). The information and knowledge economy tends to be considered in the context of 'innovation systems' which manage the interaction of production units with their environments (Dosi 1988, Malecki 1987, Kaufman and Todtling 2000), and which vary significantly between places (Cooke and Morgan 1998, Whitley 1992). Many of the factors that enable production units to harness knowledge are thought to be found in the social and institutional contexts in which they are located, rather than within production units themselves. In other words, innovation systems store knowledge independently of individuals, and facilitate learning and development through its collection, organisation and dissemination. The role of institutions is considered to be particularly important because they underpin behaviour by forming the boundaries for agents' options and choices through 'situated patterns of meaning and action' (Hasselbladh and Kallinikos 2000, 698) which manifest themselves in the form of social regularities, customs and norms.

In this respect, or so it is argued, the competitive advantage of production units located in knowledge-based environments develops in ways that are self-reinforcing. Innovative capacities evolve and adapt in response in order to accommodate particular technologies or sectors. Clusters are formed when knowledge 'spills over' from large corporations and/or universities, spawning closely-related satellite ventures in associated sectors.[3] The degree of interaction between the local academic community, businesses and financial institutions is believed to be an important building block for local innovation systems. Such interaction facilitates technological communication at the local and national levels (Castells and Hall 1994, Antonelli 2000).

These insights provide a more complete picture through which to view economic activity and represent significant progress in relation to our understanding of regional economic development. Perhaps its most meaningful contribution has been to illustrate the role and importance of institutions for social and economic systems, and for learning and innovative behaviour. As this new model has emerged, however, the role of agents appears to have been marginalised. In place of super-rational and optimising agents, we have an institution-centred approach with individuals, their behaviour, their goals and their beliefs more or less taken for granted. While knowledge and learning form central components of this approach, emphasis is placed on the role and importance of institutions in shaping cognition and action, with tacit rather than formal knowledge the primary means through which competitiveness is sustained.

Tacit knowledge reinforces the apparently pre-determined nature of behaviour because it is spread through habits and routines (which are the basis for social regularities, customs and norms), rather than through cognitive processes which require deliberation. As we pointed out in Chapter 2, institutions are considered to overwhelm individual consciousness and conflict between individuals and institutions (which in many ways underpins social change) is glossed over. By highlighting the role of tacit knowledge and routinised behaviour in innovation systems, many neo-institutionalists imply that agents are essentially receptors, and that they simply respond to their environments with little or no capacity for strategic choice. Thus in many ways, and despite its welcome critique of SEU rationality, such an approach is less of a departure from neo-classical economics and rationalist modes of thinking than it might appear. In this chapter, we redress this imbalance by placing cognition at the centre of our analysis of learning and innovation whilst acknowledging the role of inherited institutions as resources and constraints on action. *The challenge we face is to understand the development of industries and regions in terms of the thought and action of the agents that create and sustain them.*

The rapidly expanding literature on learning is indicative of the considerable interest that the subject engenders, and its presumed importance for innovation and economic performance.[4] We begin with the model created by Argyris and Schön (1978, 1996) that we have adapted slightly so that it is compatible with our views about cognition and the role of institutions, and so that it considers learning in the context of the region as well as the context of the firm. Human activity takes place on many different levels and consists of many different layers. Argyris and Schön describe this as a 'ladder of aggregation', with individual agents forming the building blocks for broader units of analysis: small groups of agents, departments, functional divisions, whole organisations, external organisations such as suppliers and distributors, and ultimately other organisations and institutions which embody regional, national and supranational social and economic systems. These layers interact in complex ways, and agents often operate on several of them simultaneously, and move frequently between them. This involves great complexity, which is magnified because each layer may have its own political 'culture' with its own (albeit related) values, norms and objectives. Both the layers, and the formal and informal structures and channels of communication that sustain them, comprise the *learning system* within which agents operate. These systems are created and sustained by agents; agents can reinforce existing patterns of learning, they can facilitate their restructuring, and they can defect from their expectations.

One of the strengths of this model is that it is agent-centred. In other words, it assumes that organisations depend on individuals to learn. This does not imply that organisations contain the sum of the knowledges of their members. The learning process is part of a complex learning cycle that consists of a number of different stages. For agents to take a proactive role in the learning process they must (1) detect error in the operation of the learning systems of which they are part; (2) search for the sources of error and devise new strategies designed to correct them; before (3) evaluating the results of the strategies that were implemented – actions obviously related to the search processes, noted above. At this point, to the extent that learning may have occurred, it has done so at an individual level. To realise learning at higher levels of aggregation, such as the firm or the region, agents must convince others of their 'discoveries, inventions and evaluations' and ultimately 'reform' the formal and informal practices of the institutions of which they are part. Organisational learning can be thus conceived as 'a process mediated by the collaborative inquiry of individual members' (Argyris and Schön 1978, p. 20).

Before we go on to outline the specifics of the model upon which our arguments are based, it is important to note that learning is not always a positive phenomenon, regardless of the level of aggregation at which it takes place.[5] Levitt and March (1988) used the term 'competency traps' to describe situations in which agents adopt patterns of behaviour that appeared to be successful at particular points in time and space, but which have been rendered outmoded. They also used the term 'superstitious learning' to describe situations where a particular decision is followed by a positive but unrelated outcome. Under these circumstances, agents may (wrongly) assume that pursuing similar actions on a related path will lead to further positive outcomes and may use the existence of a (wrongful) causal link to strengthen their positions within an organisation and region. This illustrates another facet of learning that will be discussed in more detail in a later section – that learning is a political process in which vested interests and resistance to change lead to powerful impediments to learning.

Argyris and Schön assume a tripartite learning process, with each component corresponding to a different method of detecting and correcting perceived errors, and cognitively to a different level of abstraction. *Single-loop learning* involves detecting and correcting weaknesses in behaviour based on experience (i.e. trial and error); it is a simple signal-response model of behaviour well recognised in the economics literature (see Arthur 1994 and Chapter 3). But at this level, agents do not question the assumptions and patterns of behaviour which govern aims and objectives or the procedures designed to obtain them; the purpose of single-loop learning is to achieve existing goals and objectives while ensuring that organisational performance does not move beyond current values and norms. Rules of action and standard operating procedures are often developed so that decisions are made in relation to some agreed reference point. The possibility that the values and operating norms themselves may need to be altered does not form part of the learning process. Examples of single-loop learning might include adjusting levels of output in relation to demand, or improving remuneration in order to improve staff retention.

Where existing values and norms prove adequate for meeting goals and objectives, and where goals and objectives themselves are able to sustain firm competitiveness, single-loop learning may be sufficient. In other circumstances, however, where organisational goals and objectives cannot be met within existing frameworks, or where competitive position is lost despite the attainment of a particular set of objectives, agents may be required to question more deep-rooted assumptions which may have been deliberately set aside in relation to more immediate functional objectives. The questioning of such assumptions within firms constitutes *double-loop learning*.

In addition to the detection of error with regard to effective performance in relation to existing goals, double-loop learning involves the
detection of error in relation to the assumptions that underpin
effective performance, and the nature of learning itself. Examples of
double-loop learning might include restructuring business processes
so that they are better able to adjust to changing competitive
circumstances, or reconfiguring organisation structures to improve
the flow of knowledge and information. By re-conceptualising
problems and restructuring organisational priorities and assumptions double-loop learning can be particularly effective for developing shared understanding within firms and resolving conflict
between individuals or organisational sub-units with apparently
incommensurate goals.

Triple-loop learning, also known as deutero learning, is a higher
order learning process in which agents are able to conceptualise key
facets of the modus operandi of their learning system, and influence
it accordingly, notwithstanding institutional constraints. Thus it is
primarily focused on the relationship between firms and the other
organisations that constitute their learning system. On an individual
basis, agents' capacity to change their learning system is normally
limited to the lowest rungs on the 'ladder of aggregation', such as
small groups or departments. When agents form networks and
alliances, their capacity to influence higher levels of analysis becomes
far greater. Triple-loop learning involves the capacity of agents to
operate on a higher level of abstraction, and to understand, at least in
some general sense, the learning system of which they are part, the
kinds of actions needed to engender purposeful change, as well as the
limits of such actions. Agents are required to collaborate with other
actors in order to reflect on and assess inherited systems of innovation, to consider market situations when innovation was deemed to
have been effective, and conversely, when it was deemed to have
failed. This allows agents to learn about and to articulate modes of
behaviour that facilitate and inhibit learning and innovation, to
develop and implement new strategies for innovation, and to evaluate their effectiveness. Redefining existing boundaries between different industries and services so that new niche markets emerge
(Morgan 1997), and the development of products and services based
on intrinsically new technological and/or market structures (Teece
2000) are possible examples of triple-loop learning.

In general terms, and despite significant overlap between them, different kinds of knowledge predominate for each level of learning. This is illustrated in Figure 5.1. Single-loop learning relies mainly on existing or market knowledge that is already in the organisational or regional domain. Error is corrected through established procedures, information or modes of thought, and behaviour remains within fixed boundaries. Double-loop learning is most closely associated with understanding and manipulating tacit forms of knowledge. Established patterns of thought and action, and their consequences for performance, are continually considered, questioned and articulated within firms. Solutions are developed which may represent a significant departure from the present but which are rarely at the forefront of market or technological innovation. Triple-loop learning relies mainly upon formal stores of knowledge. The relationship between organisations and their associated institutions that constitute a firm's environment or learning system is conceptualised and articulated formally between and within firms through the use of metaphors and shared frameworks. This allows firms to learn about new ideas and ways of operating, to be proactive with regard to opportunities and threats and thus at least partly shape their competitive circumstances, and ultimately to engage in innovative behaviour. Notwithstanding its simplicity, this typology provides a useful conception of the relationship between knowledge and learning.

	Single	Double	Triple
Market	**X**		
Tacit		**X**	
Formal			**X**

Figure 5.1   Levels of learning and types of knowledge

Although the distinction between double- and triple-loop learning becomes increasingly blurred during innovation (information must flow within as well as between organisations), we believe that triple-loop learning is crucial to innovation, and a defining characteristic of the information and knowledge economy. If we are correct, the implications for current thinking about economic development are highly significant; the dominant kind of knowledge underpinning innovation in the information and knowledge economy is not tacit, as is commonly assumed. It is formal and it can be learned. Indeed, Bateson (1972), the anthropologist who first developed the notion of deutero learning, described it as 'learning to learn'. Any conceptualisation of learning systems requires, of course, an understanding of their tacit components – tacit knowledge clearly plays a crucial role in any organisational or regional setting. But it is the ability to understand and articulate tacit knowledge within and between firms, and its interaction with formal knowledge, which underpins innovative behaviour. While this typology is an idealised conception of reality, it is our contention that these processes have become embedded in the institutions and behaviour of knowledge-based regions such as Silicon Valley, and has contributed significantly to the development of the information and knowledge economy. In the following section, we develop our framework in relation to knowledge-based activity.

Innovation in the information and knowledge economy

Storper (1997) provides a useful starting point for considering learning and its relationship to industrial and regional competitiveness. He argues that while 'descriptive monikers' such as post-industrial society, flexible specialisation and post-Fordism form valid, if incomplete, theoretical tools for considering economic development, the concept of learning provides the most meaningful logic for understanding sophisticated forms of economic activity capable of sustaining high wages and living standards. This is because although esoteric knowledge presents significant challenges for competitors seeking to copy and exploit it, competitive advantage in general, and knowledge in particular, is continually subject to 'powerful forces of standardisation and imitation' (p. 265) which will inevitably result in their substitution and/or relocation. This necessitates a sustained process of learning and innovation in which products and processes are continuously updated and improved so that competitiveness can be maintained. For this to happen, agents must go beyond the cycle of single-loop learning that pervades much of human behaviour, and engage in double- and triple-loop learning.

In order to understand the learning process it is not sufficient to look only at *what* agents learn. It is also necessary to examine the ways in which knowledge is acquired, shared and evaluated in the setting in which their behaviour takes place. Innovation is strongly influenced by social and institutional factors; firms and regions have their own ways of communicating and legitimising knowledge. In other words, agents' interpretations of their experiences and the meanings they attach to knowledge and learning vary between institutional and geographical contexts. In this respect, the role of institutions at all levels of aggregation is crucial.

Community networks and relational capital have long been regarded as fundamental to innovation systems. Porter (1998, 2000), probably the most influential exponent of the virtues of spatial clustering, described clusters as interconnected companies and related institutions, the relationship between which is characterised by a complex mixture of competition and cooperation.[6] Typically, clusters have vertical (customers and suppliers) and horizontal (producers of complementary products and specialist infrastructure) dimensions. Depending upon their sophistication, they might include other public and private institutions that provide specialised training, information and technical support, as well as trade associations and regulatory agencies. These actors are bound together by networks of social relationships with their own conventions and modes of expected behaviour that encourage open communication and the sharing of knowledge and information. Porter argues that clusters enhance competitiveness in a number of ways: (1) by facilitating access to specialised labour markets and superior or lower cost inputs such as components, machinery and business services; (2) by facilitating access to market, technical and other specialised knowledge and information, both explicit and tacit, which allows related firms to more easily perceive the need and opportunity for innovation; (3) by encouraging the development of complementary products and services; (4) by facilitating low-cost access to benefits such as specialised infrastructure, and advice from experts in local institutions; while (5) encouraging comparison and performance measurement in relation to local rivals.

These arguments have been articulated in more sophisticated ways by scholars such as Antonelli (2001) and Asheim (1996, 2000), and provide important insights for understanding the IKE in particular and regional development in general. Such accounts are, however, incomplete. As Malmberg and Maskell (2001) pointed out, existing theoretical analyses of spatial clustering do not explain why constituent firms are able to engage in innovative behaviour in ways that larger firms or clusters in other regions are apparently unable to replicate. In particular, they argue that much current thinking fails to articulate the processes through which competitiveness is enhanced (the sharing of knowledge and the transfer of technology), focusing instead on 'hypothetical local spill-overs', the evidence for which is the existence of the clusters themselves. The result is a 'circular causation' which fails to articulate adequately the processes involved.[7] We would further suggest that the existence of open communication channels and the resultant sharing of knowledge and information cannot *per se* account for sustained innovation over long periods given the rapidly changing market environments in which firms operate, and the powerful defensive routines (discussed below) which tend to bind agents to current patterns of thought and action. We address this lacuna by offering a prototypical framework of learning which seeks to describe and explain the complex interactions between the cognitive, institutional and organisational factors that account for the innovative behaviour that characterises the information and knowledge economy. Our framework consists of three propositions and constitutes an 'ideal type' which does not refer to specific regions or industries located in time and space. This is left to the subsequent section.

P₁: The key to learning lies in the articulation or formalisation of tacit knowledge and its relationship to explicit knowledge.[8] Argyris and Schön (1978) use the term 'theory-in-use' to describe the pictures or representations that agents build of their learning systems. Such pictures are always incomplete. Part of the learning process involves agents' endeavour to complete the picture, to conceptualise their place in relation to other actors, and to account for their actions by constructing and maintaining their social interactions. 'They [agents] try to describe themselves and their own performance insofar as they interact with others. As conditions change, they test and modify that description. Moreover, others are continually engaged in similar enquiry. It is this continual, concerted meshing of individual images of self and others, of one's own activity in the context of collective interaction, which constitutes an organisation's knowledge of its theory-in-use' (p. 16).

In order to learn and change individuals must continually question and examine existing norms and assumptions which constitute their 'theory-in-use', both informal and explicit, and the relationship between them, in response to new information, circumstances and insights. Reflexivity, by which we mean the continual framing and reframing of assumptions and norms, is the cornerstone of intelligent behaviour. Interaction and communication with other organisations and their members is a crucial component of this process because it exposes agents to new ways of working and thinking. Dialogue encourages agents to question their belief systems and to construct shared representations of the roles of different organisations and institutions at different levels of aggregation, thereby improving their understanding of their learning systems. Language allows for such interaction to take place by providing categories for agents to define their worlds and describe their experiences. However, given the socially embedded nature of meaning, it can also reinforce current patterns of thought and action because language is central to agents' beliefs, values and structures.

For these 'local traps' to be overcome, and in order to understand the diverging interpretations, aims and objectives held by the parties involved, agents must conceptualise and articulate their experiences through the use of shared metaphors, analogies, templates, mental models, concepts and frameworks. They must question how they see and think about their learning system and how its different components interact. Individuals are able to transpose what they have learned to higher levels of aggregation, both within and between firms, such as teams, departments or whole organisations through the creation of these shared systems of meaning. This is because social roles and institutions are sustained by the meaning and significance that agents attach to them, and their existence depends on their confirmation and reconfirmation by agents. We agree with Silverman (1970) that 'we reify society if we regard it as having an existence which is separate from and above the actions of men |sic|' (p. 134).

Figure 5.2 demonstrates our conception of the relationship between levels of learning and firm responses to changing circumstances. Firms that engage primarily in single-loop learning tend to be *reactive*; they allow themselves to be shaped by market and other forces and are slow to make the kind of internal adjustments necessary to reposition themselves in dynamic environments. In industries where the rate of change is particularly fast, single-loop behaviour is unlikely to be sufficient to maintain competitiveness. Firms that engage primarily in double-loop learning are always looking for new and better modes of operating, and can be characterised as *exploitative* or *adaptive*. Intra-firm patterns of behaviour are continually questioned and altered so that agents are able to take advantage of new opportunities that emerge. These firms are usually able to sustain competitiveness, but tend to be one step behind the leading firms. They are well placed to adjust to changing circumstances, but rarely influence them. By contrast, firms that engage primarily in triple-loop learning can be described as *proactive*. These are the firms that shape markets and products through new product development and new market entry. They understand the learning system of which they are part and use their ability to collaborate and develop shared meaning with other actors to define the boundaries for others.

	Single	Double	Triple
Reactive	**X**		
Exploitative/ Adaptive		**X**	
Proactive			**X**

Figure 5.2 Levels of learning and response to changing circumstances

P₂: The information and knowledge economy exists within an institutional configuration that encourages double- and triple-loop learning. Institutions have a powerful influence on learning and decision-making: their purpose is to guide action and convey expected behaviour, particularly during periods of uncertainty. Thus we can say that they have a coordinating function. In this context, we can also say that some institutional environments are more conducive to successful economic activity than others, and that the competitiveness of firms, regions and nations is profoundly affected by their inherited institutions. As implied by our first proposition, however, institutions do not form fixed boundaries for behaviour and economic activity. Agents may select, adapt or ignore aspects of their inheritance, even if inherited economic resources and knowledge and information about prospective opportunities affect their capacity to do so (see Chapter 3). In the context of the information and knowledge economy, double- and triple-loop learning processes constitute a form of relational capital. Community networks of interaction that encourage trust, the sharing of knowledge and information, and the questioning and reframing of norms and assumptions may be viewed as institutions to be reproduced from one period to the next given their contribution to long-term collective competitiveness. In some circumstances, therefore, these kinds of inherited institutional configurations may reinforce existing virtuous patterns of growth, as firms can use their strong inherited resources (locations) to more easily generate the conditions for their future success. It may seem like a paradox, but we are essentially arguing that the continual reframing of the social and institutional influences which constitute agents' learning systems itself becomes institutionalised in the information and knowledge economy, and is reinforced and confirmed through the actions of agents. This has enabled double- and triple-loop learning to become internalised and socially embedded, thereby reinforcing innovative behaviour in a cumulative manner.

Unlike many institution-centred approaches to economic development, our agent-centred model does not assume that institutions necessarily overwhelm cognitive capacity or bypass consciousness through the 'tacitness' of the information they convey. We view institutions as much more than merely shared schemas for regulating behaviour and disseminating information: they are mechanisms which are at least partly created, manipulated, refined and often discarded in order to facilitate learning and innovation. Pragmatically, of course, we accept that the extent to which social institutions can be altered, or reframed, is extremely varied; some modes of relational capital are so deep-rooted that meaningful change is exceptionally problematic. Nevertheless, we clearly prioritise cognition and meaning over institutions, rather than *vice versa.*[9]

In Figure 5.3 we illustrate the relationship between learning and institutional inheritance. Regions that are characterised mainly by single-loop learning tend to be poorly endowed with social and institutional capital. While it is possible for firms to engage in higher levels of learning in such circumstances, this is very much the exception rather than the norm. In particular, high levels of uncertainty and low levels of trust characterise relationships between firms, which tend to operate autonomously. Regions characterised mainly by double-loop learning can exist in environments that are institutionally impoverished, neutral or rich, because double-loop learning is concerned for the most part with internal adjustments and patterns of behaviour. However, it is quite unusual

	Single	Double	Triple
−ve	X	X	
~		X	
+ve		X	X

Figure 5.3 Levels of learning in the context of institutional inheritance

for regions characterised mainly by triple-loop learning to exist in institutionally impoverished environments, because triple-loop learning requires collaboration with other actors that understand the kinds of behaviour necessary for innovation. Relationships between firms are characterised by systems of shared meaning and expectations, and by a high degree of reciprocity.

P₃: Patterns of organisation encourage the sharing of knowledge and information within and between firms. Double and triple-loop learning takes place simultaneously within as well as between firms, with agents and their firms continuously making adjustments in relation to what they have learned from interaction with other actors, as their understanding of their learning system evolves and/or improves, and as agents reinterpret their circumstances and behaviour in order to develop and articulate new and better contexts for learning. In order to correct error or develop new contexts for learning, however, organisations and the production systems of which they are part tend to assume particular structures, cultures and patterns of organisation which manifest themselves explicitly in formal procedures and implicitly through routines and modes of thought.

Hierarchical and horizontal divisions within and between firms create barriers to the flow of knowledge and information. The result is sub-units that interpret common problems from different reference points. This encourages the creation of political boundaries that further inhibit learning and innovation. Considered organisationally, innovative firms tend to be characterised by limited hierarchy and levels of autonomy that empower individuals and teams (Teece 2000, 57–58). Notions of rank, seniority and functional specialisation are deemed to inhibit the flow of information and ideas, and as mechanisms that destroy unity and a shared sense of purpose. Thus decisions are taken in ways that are simple and informal, with open and responsive systems of communication and co-ordination between different parts of the organisation. Teece further suggests that innovation requires '[social] institutions with relatively low-powered incentives, where information can be freely shared without worry of expropriation, where identities can commit themselves and not be exploited by that commitment, and where disputes can be monitored and resolved in a timely way' (p. 65). Similarly, Morgan (1997) argued for the importance of autonomy and decentralisation of power and decision making: 'even though goals, objectives and targets may be helpful managerial tools, they must be used in a way that avoids the pathologies of single-loop learning; goal seeking must be accompanied by an awareness of the "limits" needed to avoid noxious outcomes; and hierarchy, design and strategic development must be approached and understood as self-organizing, emergent phenomena' (p. 117).

Morgan also noted that these firms challenge traditional premises about effective management, including strong leadership, central control, the development of clear aims and objectives, and the role of hierarchy. Such assumptions, which manifest themselves in the form of, for example, management control systems and standard operating procedures to monitor measures of performance such as sales, profit and productivity, tend to reinforce single-loop learning processes because they are designed to ensure that firms remain within predetermined boundaries. The increased use of management information systems and other IT-based monitoring systems has augmented this pattern. Argyris and Schön (1996) argued that these structures encourage agents to engage in defensive routines, 'actions and policies that are intended to protect individuals from experiencing embarrassment or threat, or the organisation as a whole from identifying the causes of the embarrassment or threat in order to correct the relevant problems' (p. 99–100). At the level of the firm, defensive routines can become embedded in formal and informal structures, norms and ways of thinking and acting.

In Figure 5.4 we have summarised the forms of industrial organisation generally associated with different levels of learning. Firms engaged in single-loop learning tend to be organised bureaucratically. Although power and responsibility may be diffused rather than centralised, this form of organisation emphasises the importance of formal and clearly defined roles and operating procedures at the expense of individual judgement. The aim is to encourage behaviour which is predictable, consistent and within current parameters. Hierarchical and functional divisions form significant barriers to the flow of information within these firms, and their relationships with external organisations tend to be rudimentary. Often, sub-cultures develop within organisations that encourage the kinds of defensive routines discussed above. By way of contrast, firms engaged in double-loop learning are organised organically. Decisions are based

	Single	Double	Triple
Bureaucratic	X		
Organic within firms		X	
Organic within & between firms			X

Figure 5.4   Levels of learning and industrial organisation

on expertise and persuasion rather than on formal roles and standard operating procedures. Where conflict arises it is resolved through formal and informal dialogue between the actors concerned, rather than through 'superiors' who occupy more senior positions. Dialogue also serves a coordinating function by allowing knowledge and information to flow throughout organisations, thereby allowing the priorities and objectives of sub-units to be understood and accommodated. Double-loop learning firms tend not, however, to be engaged in complex relationships with other actors, and so knowledge and information flows mainly within firms rather than between them.

Firms engaged in triple-loop learning tend to participate in sophisticated networks with related organisations that allow them to shape competitive circumstances and to learn new ways of operating. These firms are generally organised organically between as well as within firms. This is particularly the case for firms that develop innovative products and processes that are not compatible with existing technological and market structures. Teece (2000) calls this 'systemic innovation' and gives the examples of film-based instant photography (that required the redesign of the camera and the film), and the compact disc (which required the redesign of audio equipment and the cooperation of the music industry). It is most unlikely that a single firm (regardless of its size) could significantly reconfigure and commercialise an entire system, and so firms are required to form well-coordinated triple-loop relationships with other organisations that have complementary capabilities and capacities. In these circumstances, clear but informal channels of communication and high levels of trust are required so that knowledge and information flows as freely between firms as it does within them. This is complicated by the fact that networks may contain firms of varying sizes, resources and power, and because agents in different organisations may not interpret circumstances consistently.

Implications for European regional development

We are now in a position to consider the role and status of the information and knowledge economy in Europe. At issue here is how best to encourage European firms and regions to engage in knowledge-based activity and its associated modes of learning in order to improve competitiveness and wealth creation. Europe's social and economic institutions are characterised both by great diversity between countries and by a level of persistence at odds with corresponding US structures. Despite the apparent increasing diffusion of Anglo-American capitalism throughout continental Europe, the differences between the US and the economics of Europe remain profound. In particular, and unlike the US where the logic of profit maximisation is deeply embedded, greater emphasis is placed on the social dimensions of economic activity in continental Europe. Attempts to reconfigure aspects of Europe's economic system must take account of such differences. To apply Anglo-American modes of knowledge governance to a European context is in the first instance untenable because of the incompatible and deeply entrenched nature of existing European institutional arrangements, and in the second instance constitutes a form of intellectual imperialism which may not be acceptable to the inhabitants of Europe, many of whom remain sceptical of the 'superiority' of the US system.

We must accept, then, that European policy makers seeking to encourage knowledge-based activity operate within a set of institutional constraints, particularly with regard to the structure and performance of capital and labour markets. It is extremely unlikely that the system of labour market flexibility and venture capital that characterises the IKE in successful US regions will emerge in continental

Europe in the foreseeable future. These mechanisms are not, however, prerequisites for the IKE. Pockets of knowledge-based activity have emerged in a small number of European locations, such as Baden-Württemberg and Switzerland, albeit on relatively a modest scale by US standards.

Given the peculiarities of European capital and labour markets and our argument that a crucial facet of knowledge-based activity is double- and triple-loop learning, care must be taken in assessing the growth prospects and logic of the IKE. The key issue here is the extent to which proximity and local networks are necessary for learning and innovation. Is there any reason to suppose that so-called 'untraded interdependencies' such as co-operative behaviour between agents, and a culture of shared expectations and meaning cannot exist between agents located in different jurisdictions? It may be true, as Maskell et al. (1998) have argued, that trust and the articulation, formalisation and ultimately the transfer of tacit knowledge is more straightforward through face-to-face interaction between agents with a shared cultural heritage, and where local technological infrastructures encourage knowledge spill-overs into the local economic system. We suspect, however, that such an approach again exaggerates the importance of tacit knowledge and geography in relation to formal knowledge, and underplays the role of cognition and agents' capacity to understand the social world of which they are part. Further, and as Amin (2000) pointed out, to assume competitiveness lies mainly within local or even national production systems is to ignore evidence which indicates the prominent role of spatially elongated networks and hierarchies which cut across national boundaries. (See, for example, Dunning 1997).

Knowledge-based activity is increasingly decentralised, being re-formed into partly competing, partly complementary nodes situated in different locations around the world (see Castells 1996, McKendrick, Doner and Haggard 2000). The accelerated development of advanced transportation and communication technologies has enabled firms to coordinate more effectively their international activities. Also, the deregulation of markets and the liberalisation of trade more generally have led to an increasing number of potentially attractive investment locations. Centrifugal forces, such as the need to reduce labour and other operating costs, the need to access new markets, and the possibility of other location specific advantages such as specialist labour markets, have further encouraged information and knowledge economy production units to disperse their activities across several locations.

We agree with Amin (2000) who argues that the development of these transnational linkages has led to new corporate geographies being superimposed upon existing ones. This does not deny the central role of indigenous production units and local social capital: the most successful industrial clusters are characterised by large numbers of local production units that rely (formally or informally) upon one-another and develop into larger ones. We simply argue that knowledge-based activity is increasingly an international and decentralised activity rather than only a regional phenomenon. In any case, participation in international networks usually precipitates the emergence of new and distinctive practices and modes of operation, rather than the replacement of existing institutional arrangements by models of 'best practice' imported from other places (Gertler 2001). This is entirely consistent with our views, outlined in Chapter 2, that the interpretation of common concepts varies between locations. Agents often use bridging mechanisms, such as the common imperatives that underpin capitalism, to promote mutual understanding. But ideas and practices imported from other jurisdictions are necessarily transmutated through existing institutional structures and interpretive lenses, which are themselves modified during this process. This is what underpins social change and ensures the persistence of diversity between systems of accumulation, despite the relatively open transfer of knowledge and information between places.

This has significant implications for European regional development: 'mere' imitation or blindly copying the practices of so-called exemplar regions will ensure that European levels of competitiveness remain below those of its currently more successful rivals, such as the US, for the foreseeable future. Only by learning about the virtues of other systems and marrying these to Europe's existing strengths, can it hope to leapfrog the US and establish itself as a model for others. In this context, double- and triple-loop learning provides a powerful reference point with which to view innovation and economic development. We suggest that the growth of the information and knowledge economy in Europe could be linked in part to external forces, with multinational corporations, which have been instrumental in the growth of industrial districts around the world, playing a crucial part. In the previous section we outlined three propositions in relation to successful knowledge-based activity. In the remainder of this section we look at these in turn in the context of European regional development.

P₁: The key to learning lies in the articulation or formalisation of tacit knowledge and its relationship to explicit knowledge. This is a process that needs to be carried out within and between organisations, and European firms need to be more proactive in this respect. Agents at all levels must learn to appreciate the complexity and diversity of the issues they face, and to recognise, absorb and manage this complexity. To understand and articulate tacit knowledge, individuals, teams, and other units must be 'empowered to find innovations around local issues and problems that resonate with their needs. This also provides a resource for innovation within the broader organisation, as the variety and innovation thus experienced is shared and used as a resource for further learning' (Morgan 1997, p. 113). We envisage a shared decision-making process where agents transfer information, insights and ideas, and where consensus and shared meaning emerges from interaction, rather than being imposed by hierarchies with vested interests in maintaining the status quo. Decisions, and the values and norms that underpin them, need to be explored from different angles so that courses of action that satisfy multiple perspectives and concerns can be developed.

This takes us back to the crux of our argument about human behaviour: while agents are, at one level, social beings moulded in thought and action by their environments, they have the capacity to operate at a higher level of abstraction, to make judgements about how the different parts of their learning system fit together, to take action to engender meaningful change, and to make judgements about the limits of such action. In other words, agents in European firms need to learn to learn.

P₂: The IKE exists within an institutional configuration that encourages double- and triple-loop learning. Management theory has traditionally stressed the importance of organisational design and structure for sustaining and improving competitiveness. Our model envisages an alternative source of competitive advantage: language, values, social interaction and the exchange of ideas. As noted above, European firms are faced with the challenge of developing systems of shared meaning, encouraging their members to question the current para-meters within which their behaviour is evaluated by others, and developing strategies for action that take into account the structure and limits of the learning system of which they are part.

For this to happen in a sustained fashion, new kinds of thinking need to become transposed onto the structures and modes of opera-tion of organisations and other institutions which constitute their environments. We see this partly as a challenge of cultural change: the introduction of new forms of technology, organisation and operating procedures are necessary but insufficient for the emer-gence of distinctive patterns of learning. We recognise, of course, that cultural change is highly problematic. But unless we can suggest ways of introducing double- and triple-loop learning into the European context, we cannot move beyond the circular argu-ments of which we were critical earlier in this chapter. We consider the participation of European firms in spatially-elongated networks of knowledge-based activity to be crucial, because this will expose agents in European jurisdictions to new modes of thinking and acting. These networks are presently located mainly in the US. However, our model of institutional change allows for the introduc-tion of new ideas and modes of thought which are compatible with existing structures. These ideas will take new and unpredictable forms that may allow European firms and regions to move beyond existing models of best practice. This should generate a momentum which is self-reinforcing: the presence of even small numbers of internationally competitive firms in a given region or production system can contribute significantly to the competitiveness of other firms by acting as role models and sources of ideas for them.

P_3: Patterns of organisation encourage the sharing of knowledge and infor-mation within and between firms. Few aspects of the American capital-ist model have been so influential as the bureaucratic, hierarchical and vertically integrated form of industrial organisation. The appli-cation of scientific management (the separation of management's thought from labour's doing) and the development of the multidivi-sional form of organisation was seen by Alfred Chandler and his

acolytes as the cornerstone of American economic hegemony in the period following the Second World War. While many European countries were slow to adopt these practices and their associated ideas, there can be little doubt that they have been very influential in the post-war development of European industrial and economic structures, and economic development more generally. It is surely ironic that the flexible specialisation advocated by Piore and Sabel (1984), a form of which now permeates the information and knowledge economy in the US, was widespread in parts of Europe prior to 1945, but was at least partly rejected in favour of horizontally and vertically integrated corporations which were influenced by 'scientific' approaches to management because of the apparent superiority of the US system. (See McKinlay and Zeitlin 1986 and Ackroyd and Lawrenson 1996 for the case of the UK).

We noted earlier that we believe the creation of new forms of management and organisation is in many respects a challenge of cultural change. It involves creating systems of meaning that are shared by agents at all levels and who accept, internalise and act upon them. Thus innovation requires that organisations have a 'holographic' quality (Morgan 1997), with the attributes of the whole transposed onto its constituent parts. This involves a particular form of organisation: 'The best teams, and the free-flowing organisations that have discarded bureaucratic forms of management, constantly reflect this quality. They are organised through core meanings that people own and share. It is this quality that allows them to be flexible, adaptive and non-bureaucratic. Organisationally, shared meanings provide alternatives to control through external procedures and rules' (p. 143). Although the advantages of democratic forms of organisation is well known, particularly for firms operating in turbulent environments, the extent to which such forms are widespread is less clear. Without open channels of communication and flat hierarchies that allow agents to share their experiences within and between organisations, it is difficult to envisage how the first two propositions can be achieved.

Conclusions

In this chapter, we have argued that conventional explanations of the information economy often fall short. Most obviously, there is a temptation to ascribe causal significance to the clustering of activities in certain regions supposing that an essential prerequisite for building a knowledge economy is the existence of such clusters; there remains an unresolved question of whether clustering is a cause or an effect of the information economy. Also important, however, is the realisation that common understandings in the regional development literature about the nature of learning (the translation of information into knowledge) are at best rudimentary and at worst rather unsophisticated in the light of parallel debates in the management sciences concerning the modes and mechanisms of learning and knowledge acquisition. In this chapter, one goal has been to articulate a more complete model of learning and knowledge acquisition relying upon models of cognition and search that can be attributed, in part, to the early work of Simon and Arygris and Schön. From these models, we have advanced (we hope) a more nuanced account about the possible implications of the knowledge economy for European regional development.

In making our assessment, we have been guided by two rather basic suppositions drawn from our knowledge of contemporary Anglo-American and European circumstances. In the first instance, we are very conscious of the fact that Europe is a very different economic environment to its Anglo-American brothers and sisters. The commonplace expectations about capital market and labour market flexibility that are so important to the Anglo-American world are rarely matched in European nations and regions. Europe is dominated by that which was inherited from the immediate post-war settlement, and various competing conceptions about the nature and significance of culture, society, and the proper relationship between economy and civil society. In the second instance, we are also very conscious of the fact that Silicon Valley and similar kinds of regional systems of innovation exist – to imagine that the proper response is to build competing clusters of innovation in continental Europe seems at best a long-term prospect and at worst a forlorn hope. We should, however, look for ways that European industry might take advantage of the existence of Silicon Valley to build institutions and encourage entrepreneurship that is able to systematically leapfrog Anglo-American initiatives.

In other words, we are less convinced that the knowledge economy is essentially a geographical phenomenon than we are convinced that the knowledge economy is a distinctive form of learning utilising intellectual capital in mutually reinforcing institutional environments. Of course, we appreciate the fact that these kinds of environments may be local in ways consistent with the Marshallian industrial districts of the 19ᵗʰ century and regions such as the Third Italy of the 20ᵗʰ century. But we would also contend that if Europe is to leapfrog the Anglo-American world in terms of its innovative potential it cannot wait for a new Silicon Valley in Europe. Surely the immediate future must be the formation of learning environments that bring together in virtual spaces the intellectual potential of European industry. The contrast we wish to draw here is between localised centres of innovation and spatially elongated centres of innovation that rely upon advanced communication technologies and moments of interaction that achieve the same result: 'centres' of innovation that spin-out ideas into the market place thereby contributing to the long-term growth of capital accumulation and labour productivity (contra Saxenian 1994).

Our analysis of the learning process drew distinctions between simple and more complex conceptions of reflexivity. So much of the literature is preoccupied with what is termed single-loop learning (signal-response) or possibly double-loop learning (response and adjustment) that analysts often miss the importance of so-called triple-loop learning (learning to learn). At the same time, many analysts tend to treat institutions and regions as entities that can learn ignoring the fact that it is individual agents who are the locus of cognitive capacity. We do not dispute the significance of institutions and regions for the learning process; in the best of worlds, these entities are extremely valuable resources for facilitating and economising upon the learning process. They embody all kinds of useful heuristics and templates that allow for the translation of decisions into actions. But equally institutions and regions can be impossible burdens upon agents' imagination and innovation (see chapter 3). The interaction between agents and their environments determines the growth potential of the information economy.

But we must be cautious about their interaction. Agents are more than their environments. They learn, they develop mechanisms for learning, and they often fail to recognise their own mistaken choices and those of their colleagues. Agents need not benefit from their environments nor necessarily contribute to the growth potential of their environments. Indeed, many institutional and regional circumstances, whether Anglo-American or European, seem irrelevant to the growth potential of their citizens. Too many environments are resource-poor, are paralysed by political consensus seeking, and are merely instruments of government policy. We have many examples of these cases but, unfortunately, we have few instances of so-called successful regions. Silicon Valley and Rt 128 Boston and other similar places have become emblems or symbols of success rather than real examples of the scope of potential interaction between learning and the knowledge economy. More important than regions, we would argue, is a better understanding of cognitive capacity, decision-making, and how and why knowledge is so essential to the information and knowledge economy.

In this respect, we argue for a shift in focus from tacit knowledge (the presumed engine of innovation) to the ways in which knowledge is formalised, revised and adapted to changing circumstances. We argue that tacit knowledge cannot be the source of innovation. And we argue that tacit knowledge is always incremental rather than developmental. Organising systems of triple-loop learning is essential to the growth of the information economy in Europe and elsewhere. We do not underestimate the difficulty of this kind of institution-building. But we are convinced that institutions or regions by themselves are neither necessary nor sufficient for the process of innovation. By contrast managing cognition, building ready mechanisms of response and change are necessary conditions for the information and knowledge economy.

6
Global Competitiveness

In this book we have sketched the rudiments of a theoretical approach to global and regional economic competitiveness. We have done so in the context of a multidisciplinary approach to globalisation, regional economic development, and competitive strategy inside and outside of firms, industries, and regions. We have taken advantage of the explosion of literature on these topics over the past 10 to 15 years, noting where we agree and disagree with the dominant arguments currently expressed at the intersection between global economic integration and local economic change. We have been especially conscious of the literature in economic geography, but have also sought to recognise the relevant contributions from management studies, sociology and political economy. We have done so in order to address in a comprehensive way a vital intersection in economic life, one that promises to dominate everyday life through much of the 21st century.

Our arguments about global economic integration and local economic change have been informed by reference to the early work by Herbert Simon and his colleagues on modes of decision-making. The Carnegie School was a moment in intellectual history when commonplace assumptions made about rational decision-making were exposed to close analytical scrutiny and empirical study about the plausibility of 'rational actor' models in the real world. Although widely recognised, this body of work has not been exploited as we believe it should have been given all the implications that can be drawn about the relationship between agent decision-making and the contexts or environments in which people find themselves. For us, this has an immediate and obvious geographical resonance. But equally, for those concerned about the place of economic agents in a world of institutions, regions and industries, the work of Herbert Simon looms large methodologically and conceptually. Throughout the book, we have tackled contemporary issues in the light of the lessons to be drawn from a self-conscious understanding of the cognitive capacities and relationships between agents and their environments.

We began the project very much aware of the profound global competitive pressures facing firms and places. This is most obvious, of course, in Western Europe and the emerging continental European economy (adding in central and Eastern Europe). But it has been plain for those whose experience is of Latin America and north-east Asia over the last decades. For the European nation-state, economic integration whether European or global is a very real threat to their fiscal and monetary autonomy, the path and performance of their national economies, and the place of their regions in an economic world that seems to have fewer boundaries, more prospects for growth and expansion, but also more rivals and competitors. The European nation-state is curiously in-between the global and the local, seeking ways to fashion a future for itself and its citizens at risk to economic competition. In this context, inherited institutions and 'embedded' relationships appear to be constraints on competitiveness rather than the means of enhancing agents' decision-making. This may seem harsh opinion, at odds with many analysts of the European 'project'. There appears to be a rearguard action being fought by those who wish to protect nation-state institutions and relationships from emerging new centres of power, both globally and locally.

These issues have become the lifeblood of academic and policy related research focused upon global competitiveness and economic geography. These issues are also enmeshed with the arguments made in each chapter of this book. We don't need at this stage to re-run the key arguments. Rather, in the final chapter of the book we take stock of our arguments and look forward to broader issues that are part of an expansive agenda for future research. This research concerns both academic argument and debate, and individual and collective futures. Globalisation has many critics. Globalisation is also a roller coaster of events, and their transmission through international capital markets and local labour markets. In this respect, it may be that the current consensus in favour of globalisation is derailed by catastrophic economic circumstances. But whatever the anxieties and concerns, we think it more likely that globalisation will be the framework for economic growth over the 21st century. In that case, academic research has much to learn and, in the end, we hope has much to offer those seeking a better understanding of the global economy.

If so, the research agenda for the social sciences must be transformed. For too many years, the agenda has been preoccupied with nation-state policy concerns, transfixed by parochial interests and the immediate debate about who benefits and who loses from public policy and market based decision-making. There are many issues that have to be rethought, conceptually and empirically. For example, how are we to conceptualise social justice in a world in which the nation-state is caught between agents located in regional economies reaching out into the global economy and global economic actors penetrating into the very fabric of 19th and 20th century nation states? Consider another question: how should we conceptualise the commitments and obligations of so-called 'local' economic agents in relation to their peers located elsewhere within the nation-state notwithstanding the fact that their fellow citizens may be irrelevant to their long-term economic well-being? At this point, the local and the global may be transformed into a sweeping set of flows and relationships that are in fact trans-national rather than national.

In this chapter, we can hardly answer these questions or in fact even provide ready-made templates for their study. Nevertheless we do think that the questions raised throughout the book and the arguments used to consider these questions may have important implications for reaching into a world that seems, paradoxically, to be increasingly diverse *and* integrated. In this chapter we recount crucial points of departure in making our arguments, we discuss the changing academic and policy conceptions of regional and economic development, and examine briefly the relevance of the knowledge economy for global and regional competitiveness.

Four points of departure

Let us now summarise the crucial points of departure that informs arguments throughout the book. Our intention here is to be crudely general; to summarise and be argumentative about how we have proceeded and how others might wish to understand the challenges posed by the book. In doing so, we hope the points of departure are a recognition of what we have learnt from existing literature relevant to the project. In this section we make four distinct arguments set out in the form of propositions.

P_1: *The study of competitiveness and the local and the global requires a non-idealistic approach to agent decision-making.* That is, many social scientists presume that agents are rational actors in the sense that they (agents) are assumed to take as given the context in which decision-making occurs while seeking to optimise outcomes with respect to their preferences and tastes. What if *context* is not given? What if there is a close, even intimate, connection between context, agent attitudes and preferences, and hence agent decision-making? Idealism whether social-theoretical or normative has a limited place in a world that is in flux. Of course, it is one way of holding constant a changing world. But when used as a methodological template for the study of competitiveness and globalisation, the rational actor model is a cul-de-sac rather than a way forward.

Notice, of course, that although non-idealistic our approach nevertheless relies upon a fairly crude and at times simple conception of cognitive capacity and psychological competence. One lesson we have learnt in building an argument against the rational actor model is that there is much more to be learnt about the psychological roots of agent decision-making than we have been able to consider in this book. At one level, we have been most impressed with recent developments in the psychology of decision-making, particularly those that take seriously agents' tendencies to economise on the costs of decision-making while recognising the risks and uncertainty associated with a changing world. At another level, however, we are astonished at the sweeping and uncritically assessed generalisations made about agents' motivations, and where evolutionary metaphors are invoked to explain in a tactical sense behaviour that must be deeply affected by social and cultural associations rather than obscure and remotely located elements of our gene structure and DNA.

P₂: The study of global competitiveness must take seriously history and geography in relation to agent decision-making. Too often, it appears that those concerned about the intersection between agents and places ultimately choose one or the other as the driving force behind observed outcomes. Having been focused on explaining their interaction throughout the book, we are sympathetic to the difficulties encountered by those who intend to take agents and history and geography seriously; indeed, critics of separate chapters and papers have suggested that for all our argument in favour of history and geography we remain unabashedly agent focused.

There is an important point in such criticism: conceptually we do think that agents have priority over history and geography in the sense that agents have consciousness, agents learn, and agents make decisions. To think otherwise is to imagine that history and geography have together or separately an autonomous motive force or long term 'objective'. We do not believe that this is credible as an intellectual assumption or as a practical reality. However, it is obvious that if agents are best characterised as subject to cognitive limits and complex psychological motives, history and geography are not just the stage upon which they act, history and geography are the resources (or not) at hand for agents self conscious of their incapacities as decision-makers. We make mistakes. We knowingly make mistakes. And we try to guard against the costs of those mistakes either at the point of decision-making or subsequent to decision-making through incremental adjustments of strategy and response. We do so in the context of history and geography that provide us with social resources to help in decision-making just as history and geography may provide us with impossible burdens that overwhelm any sense of autonomy and purpose.

P₃: The study of global competitiveness should recognise that market signals and behavioural responses are far more complex than often assumed. The most common model of agent decision-making is one based upon a fairly simple signal-response model of impulse and communication (signal) and interpretation and action (response). Curiously, this model does not require any self-conscious assessment by agents of either the quality or quantity of the signal or indeed their own capacity to understand and appreciate its meaning. In other words, this particular model of decision-making is not a model of decision-making at all; it is a model based upon a black box where the input (signal) is somehow transformed into an output (response). We could be talking about pigeons as much as humans when using the model. Neglected is human beings' self-consciousness, sense of self in relation to their environment, and their appreciation of the multiple levels of other agents' strategic actions which must surely feature in any conception of decision-making.

We make this argument in some detail in our chapter on path dependence. We do not mean to suggest that we have developed a fully-fledged alternative going beyond signal-response behaviour to self-consciousness, reflexivity, and multiple levels of expectation and consciousness. But it is crucial to emphasise that if we are to take seriously agents' self consciousness we must also take seriously how agents' thoughts and actions are framed and structured by their contexts. In other words, we must take seriously the process whereby agents frame their interpretation of market events and how that framing process is linked and informed by their place amongst other agents. In some ways, of course, the research on networks is an attempt to make sense of that kind of decision-making. But, too often, the signal-response model is replaced with a model of local (or sometimes global) networks which simply replace agents with networks without an articulation of the black box. To illustrate, there are few studies about the advantages and disadvantages of clustered location in relation to strategic market behaviour.

P_4: *The study of global competitiveness should be sensitive to the process whereby agents learn and adjust their actions (or do not adjust their actions) in relation to what they have learned or not learned.* Unfortunately, in making this argument it could be suggested that we are (as many others are) simply replacing one model with another model, in this case called 'learning' in all its local and global manifestations (as surveyed in, for example, the *Oxford Handbook of Economic Geography*). In fact, we are alarmed and uneasy about the 'learning' argument if all that we have done is to join a stream of research that has as its ultimate conclusion the claim that learning enhances competitiveness, the place of the region in the global economy, and thereafter the rate of economic growth. At one time, export led models of economic growth dominated economic theory and whole countries' economic strategies. This is being replaced in one form or another by models of endogenous growth that have at their base a theory of economic growth dependent upon the capitalisation of learning. Indeed, there is an industry managed by consultants wherein 'the learning region' has become the litmus test of relevance and innovation.

As is obvious from the penultimate chapter of this book, we do think that learning is a vital ingredient in any theory of agent-based decision-making. However, we also think that learning is far more problematic than many others would seem to have us believe. For us, the problems of decision-making (cognitive capacity, self consciousness, and the regulation of errors) do not suddenly disappear by virtue of the fact that agents learn. Quite the contrary, it seems that the problems we have identified in 'signal-response' models of decision-making are much the same as the problems now apparent in the 'learning' models of decision-making. We know very little in fact about how agents learn, how that learning process is or is not goal directed, and whether learning changes actions or expectations in systematic and non-systematic ways. We do know that human beings use heuristics – shorthand methods of economical decision-making, based partly upon experience and intuition, recognising that accuracy is more often than not less important than being approximately correct in circumstances that allow for subsequent revision and adjustment.

Regional development – past and present

There was a time, not so long ago, when regional economic development was a question of the allocation of national employment. Large firms, large industries, their employment practices and their location decisions were the reference points for the relevant literature and for nation-state policy makers. So, for example, a great deal of research was focused upon the geographical consequences of different stages in the product life-cycle; from invention, to innovation, and to mass-production, regions were thought to have a distinctive place in the transformation of ideas into products. 'Place' was located with reference to the nation state, the location decisions of multinational firms, and the emergence of new local and global sites of production. Early editions of Peter Dicken's *Global Shift* were all about this kind of dynamic. While the literature focused upon North America and Western Europe, it became an important conceptual logic in understanding the landscape of production in north-east and south-east Asia. It remains one of a number of themes that occur and re-occur in debate about the prospects for regional economic development.

In this context, regional economic development was about the rationing of jobs between more or less deserving regions. Eligible regions had to meet certain criteria: for example, high levels of unemployment, low relative incomes and lower rates of economic growth as reflected in employment growth. Having attained eligibility, such regions were then provided with the appropriate infrastructure and capital development projects consistent with the introduction of multi-plant firms whose role and responsibility was to bring mass industrialisation to the 'backward' region. In doing so, roads, railways, airports, and other related communication networks were deemed essential. Later on, electronic access to international high-speed and high quality communication links also played a part in matching-up the attributes of regions with their incoming employment providers. The transfer of production jobs into depressed regions was the ultimate goal of regional policy.

Global competitiveness was thus seen to be an attribute of regional infrastructure and an attribute of the firms that could be attracted to such regions. Once established, global competitiveness was also a function of the skills and productive qualities of the indigenous workforce. In the end, retaining large employers in such regions has become as much a question of managing local productivity as it was a matter of having the physical and capital infrastructures necessary to sustain the links between the region, the nation and the international economic system. These kinds of regional economic development policies, and especially production and related relocation subsidies, have fallen out of favour and are no longer consistent with WTO and European Union expectations, notwithstanding the fact that there remains a long term adverse map of employment opportunities across North America, Europe, and indeed the globe. What has changed, of course, is that multinational firms have systematically increased labour productivity in their existing production units, adopted advanced technologies consistent with much higher levels of productivity in the future, and have generally downsized their employment bases. There is no doubt we can still find 'Fordist' factories; but we have to go to Asia and Latin America to find the last remnants of industrial and corporate revolution of the early 20th century.

The industrial engines of nation-state economic development such as automobile manufacturing, clothing, textiles and apparel production, and electrical and electronic component parts (so often the subject of academic research throughout Western economies), are now less obvious 'solutions' to problems of regional economic development. This is not to say that foreign direct investment is less important in Europe or for that matter North America. There are stand-out examples where foreign direct investment in production facilities has had enormous consequences for nation-state and regional growth trajectories (witness the case of Ireland; see O'Sullivan 2002). But it is just as clear that across Europe and North America these industries are the object of corporate and industrial restructuring – the destruction of jobs – rather than continued growth and decentralisation of production facilities. Employment opportunities in these industries and regions have shrunk as national markets have become open to production sites in other nations and their regions where the costs of production are incomparably lower. In these ways, globalisation has brought important employment opportunities to many regions of the developed world but has also put enormous pressure on local, nation-state, and supranational institutions and their capacity to innovate and invest in new ideas and new forms of production.

Hence the current obsession with endogenous economic growth, entrepreneurial clusters, and regions of learning and innovation. Indeed, there has been a most remarkable intellectual and conceptual transformation wherein national economic growth, instead of being allocated down to the regions is now seen to be dependent upon having regions of innovation which can contribute to national economic well-being. From the top-down allocation of jobs to regions we now find that regions are the building blocks of national and indeed pan-European and North American economic growth. Not surprisingly, there is an enormous market for inventories of regional potentials, just as there appears great concern about the relevance of nation-state institutions to what is otherwise seen to be a very local phenomenon. Consequently, regions have become centres of expertise and innovation apparently not available at the scale of the nation state. At the limit, a question asked of many national policy makers is whether they have sufficient regional diversity – a most remarkable transformation of the status of regions with respect to the nation-state over the past 20 or so years.

At the same time, the unit of analysis has changed enormously. From large firms, from the modern corporation and its analysts such as Chandler and Galbraith, and from manufacturing industries we have witnessed a realignment of argument and opinion to small and medium enterprises, invention and innovation, and products and processes rather than monolithic blocks of whole industries and nations. In this regard, there appears to be increasing heterogeneity within so-called industrial sectors and greater uncertainty about the future sources of invention and innovation, notwithstanding the apparent dominance of the United States over the 1990s. Large firms still exist. And there seems little likelihood of their claim on national and global imagination declining – there remains a vital and enormously powerful world of large firms and financial institutions and instruments that have the capacity to sweep over the entire global economic landscape. The point we would make here is that their capacity to innovate and bring new products and processes into the global economy depends increasingly on their capacity to develop local partnerships and alliances, but that these links are less tangible and less secure than during much of the last century.

Regional economic development in the early years of the 21st century is about rediscovering economic agency, the place of economic agents in local and global economies, and the mix of resources necessary to facilitate their development from local players into global opportunists. In this respect, concepts such as *path dependence, embeddedness,* and the *continuity of diversity* seem tangential to local and global growth potentials. Perhaps this is because these concepts resonate with the accumulated history and geography of past modes of production. Put slightly differently, it is arguable that competitiveness and the local and the global are about transforming history and geography into either something entirely benign or, hopefully, something that can add value to economic agents' global competitive strategies. By contrast, there is a sense in which concepts such as path dependence and embeddedness are better able to explain why economic agents persist with less competitive strategies than that which they might adopt; likewise, embeddedness may help explain local productivity profiles better than more conventional concepts such as human capital. But do path dependence and embeddedness as facts of life have the flexibility or openness to accommodate agent defection and agent transformation beyond their local milieu? The world of networks seems to be a way out of path dependence and embeddedness. But as we have mentioned above, the introduction of networks as a means of liberation and transformation runs the danger of being basically empty of content unless we can develop a deeper understanding of their nature and content.

The future geography and functional typology of economic activity is more open than ever before. We find it difficult to imagine that we will go back to large firms and large industries astride regions, nations, and the international economy. We also find it improbable that path dependence and embeddedness will remain constraints upon corporate strategy in a world of industrial restructuring (of existing productive infrastructure) and ever-embracing competition. More than ever before, regions of innovation are both the destination of foreign direct investment and the source of new products and processes diffused across the globe. We find it hard to imagine that there will be just a handful of such regions. We find it more credible to imagine that clusters of innovation will become geographically far more inclusive than hitherto. We also find it difficult to imagine that nation-states will have much to offer in the way of policy-making potential. More likely, the economics of landscape of tomorrow will be dominated by regional development potentials facilitated by nation-state institutions such as education, finance, and population diversity and growth (Florida 2002), but where such institutions play less significant roles.

There is a danger, however, that more inclusive and internationally diverse clusters of innovation fail to fulfil their potential in supporting the development of regions with high levels of unemployment and social exclusion and low rates of growth. This applies to both developed and developing economies. Imagine a knowledge intensive firm in Poland that develops close ties with suppliers, venture capitalists and research institutions from across the globe. There is no need, indeed there is no incentive, for such a firm to build alliances with local actors in order to achieve its objectives. By taking advantage of advanced communication technologies this firm could successfully grow and develop without participating in or relying upon a local infrastructure. In such a scenario, there is very little in the way of *local* capacity building, the firm in question contributing in only a limited way to economic development within Poland. Global linkages of this kind will not allow for effective local economic development in peripheral regions unless firms are able to develop local *and* global networks simultaneously.

The knowledge economy of the 21st century

We have observed that as globalisation accelerates, local and national markets in the developed world are increasingly vulnerable to penetration by competitors located in low cost regions. In this context, policy makers across Western economies look to knowledge intensive as opposed to labour intensive activities for future industry and employment involving products and services which are not easily subject to standardisation, imitation, substitution and/or relocation (Storper 1997). At the Lisbon meeting of first ministers, the EU declared that Europe is to be the leading knowledge economy of the 21st century. To do so will require remarkable political will as much as it will require far-sighted economic imagination. Most obviously, it requires rethinking regional economic development, and movement away from the allocation of employment to fostering geographical and industrial clusters of innovation. It requires, as well, enormous political resilience in the face of the claims made by vested interest groups for their share of employment in the automobile industry, the steel industry, labour intensive manufacturing in general, and related vestiges of the Fordist economy of the 20th century. Reaction and resistance to economic change and the imperatives of globalisation are especially important features of contemporary nation-state politics. Brought together are those adversely affected by changing employment and community opportunities with those on the far left and far right who have much to gain by exploiting social alienation. The knowledge economy is in this respect a threat to the world inherited from the past, but something that must be embraced if economic growth is to serve the interests of those disaffected by change.

The knowledge economy is also a set of processes and opportunities less radical than many might suppose. For example, consider that a crucial component of the knowledge economy is the application of high-quality communication networks to production systems. One of the most remarkable transformations of the past 25 years has been in systems of distribution, both between businesses and between businesses and consumers. Using communication technologies combined with electronic tracking systems, European industry has been brought together in a virtual sense but also in a quite tangible sense as illustrated by the vastly expanded networks of road and rail transport logistics. This is not a revolution but a series of incremental steps towards a pan-European integrated network of production, distribution, and consumption. At one level, the geography of production has largely remained the same but at another level geography has been stitched together in ways that will facilitate rationalisation of existing productive capacity. This may not be the knowledge economy of Silicon Valley but it is the knowledge economy which is the means of integration.

The knowledge economy of the 21st century is also about innovation applied to production systems themselves. Here, common goals include enhancing labour productivity while sustaining high levels of product quality and reliability. Producers have been interested in both the cost effectiveness of production systems and the reputation of their products, supposing that their combination will be sufficient to protect market share while providing a means of penetrating other markets developed and less developed. For the largest firms, such technologies are the result of their own research and development, the transfer of technology between units of the firm across the world, and their application to local circumstances drawing upon distinctive sets of organisational and skill attributes (Gertler 2001). For much smaller firms without the luxury of internal research and development, the application of technology to production is all about finding the appropriate sources of innovation in cost-effective ways. Alliances, networks, partnerships, and close links between suppliers and consumers are vital mechanisms which facilitate the collection of relevant information and the transfer of knowledge. At the core of these kinds of processes is learning: for large firms, mutual learning amongst related but often distant units is one source of innovation while for smaller firms learning from others, including those that may be rivals, is a vital element of the knowledge economy.

As indicated above, learning can be seen as a process of information collection, information assessment, and the application of related technologies to the production process. In that case, there may well be a clear connection between inputs and outputs which takes the form of a measurable link allowing for evaluation of competing technologies with respect to their consequences for labour productivity and product quality. As described, learning seems to be an entirely logical and organised process with established parameters setting agent decision-making and those aspects to be considered and those to be discarded as irrelevant in the search for competitiveness. However, a massive and extensive literature has developed over the past decade showing that agent decision-making, learning, and the application of new technology is a far more problematic process than the rational actor model would have us believe. In part, there are issues of agent-institution competence and responsibility. And there are issues, in a broader sense, of corporate governance whether between managers (up and down the hierarchy) or between owners and managers (between shareholders and stakeholders). These are issues of organisational flexibility. But they are also issues about the relative performance of whole systems of economic organisation (see, for example, Dore 2000).

These issues are widely debated inside and outside of economic geography. But, as we have come to realise, the connection between learning and knowledge is even more problematic than this simple sketch suggests. It also presumes an understood connection between cause and effect. The previous discussion presumes that a crucial question in this regard has to do with the social organisation of production systems within and between firms, whether located together or at a distance from one another. We have, in the terms introduced in the previous chapter of this book, discussed these issues with reference to single-, double- and triple-loop learning. However, one of the most problematic aspects of the learning and knowledge economy is surely the fact that any presumption in favour of well-defined cause and effect relationships must be viewed with great suspicion. In many cases, particularly in circumstances where information is in short supply and decisions have to be made on the basis of judgment and instinct, cause and effect relationships may be too abstract to be definitive. In that case, the knowledge economy is also about how agents make and re-make decisions in the context of risk and uncertainty.

The knowledge economy of the 21st century will be a most demanding environment. Success will be measured by flexibility in relation to the management of risk and uncertainty, more so than just the adoption and implementation of new technology. Systems of learning will have to become systems of accommodation, providing agents and institutions with sufficient discretion to make the best possible decisions in circumstances where cause and effect relationships are at best abstract and at worst forever in flux. Systems of learning may be local in the sense that they are informal rather than formal, coalitions rather than government institutions, and open rather than closed. In that case, the knowledge economy of the 21st century will be built around agent-based decision-making rather than imposed from nation-state or even pan-European regulations.

By this account, global and regional competitiveness depends upon the relationship between agents, their environments, and their capacity for mutual learning and coalition formations. As we have suggested throughout the book, agent-based decision-making is far more problematic than hitherto acknowledged. The intellectual agenda for the 21st century is to better understand agent-based decision-making in a world of global and regional competition without the idealism that has so impoverished our conceptual and practical tool kits.

Notes

Chapter 1   Introduction

1. Reinert uses the Haitian baseball industry to illustrate his point. Despite being the most efficient manufacturer of baseballs in the world with the largest share of the international market, the profits of Haitian baseball manufacturers are relatively small and the standard of living of their employees is extremely low.

2. Witness, for example, the value now associated with geographical clusters of innovation like Silicon Valley (Saxenian 1994). Also, see Cooke (2001) for a discussion of the innovation gap between the US and Europe, Bresnahan, Gambardella and Saxenian (2001) for a compelling account of cluster formation in successful regions in different parts of the world, Feldman (2001) for an excellent case study of the growth and development of the US Capitol region, and Owen-Smith et al. (2002) for an interesting comparison of the development of the biomedical industries in the US and Europe.

3. See Fujimoto (1999) for a discussion of the emergence of a learning system in the context of a complex and sophisticated manufacturing environment.

4. This objection is in fact a series of rather different objections coming from a variety of quarters. For example, those who suggest that we attribute too much significance to decision-making could come from conventional economic theory arguing that efficient markets impose a kind of discipline on economic agents' decision-making. The implication being, of course, that so-called 'irrational' behaviour and decision-making is stripped away by virtue of the arbitrage processes inherent in market capitalism. This is clearly not quite the same objection as those who would argue that social structure and the distribution of political power are more obviously the dominant forces driving economic outcomes. Whatever economic agents' own particular interests and criteria for decision-making, this kind of argument supposes that any focus upon economic agents is less relevant than a comprehensive and historically informed analysis of whole societies, their institutions and organisation. At this point, we do not wish to adjudicate between arguments within this basic objection.

5. We believe economic agents' decisions in matters such as competitive strategy and investment are very important in understanding the evolution and trajectory of local communities, regions and whole nation-states. We find it difficult to accept claims suggesting otherwise; the efficient market hypothesis, for example, is surely open to debate from

those with the specialised theoretical and financial armoury necessary to dispute it as a practical reality (compare Shiller 2000 and Shleifer 2000 with Jensen 1998).

Chapter 2   Agents and Institutions

1. For many researchers, comparative study was driven by a combination of individual research interests and disciplinary imperatives. Looking across the social sciences it could be contended, as did Lipset (1963, 1990), that the guiding principle underpinning this work was an assumption that comparative study allows one to better understand the similarities between peoples as well as what is unique about the institutions and cultures of countries.
2. The EU has tended to fund research in science and engineering rather than social science, and it is only relatively recently that the latter has formed part of the EU's research agenda. Indeed, it is hard to avoid the conclusion that the EU continues to prioritise scientific and engineering-based research over and above social scientific research, as reflected in their respective budgets. Thus the money available for social and economic research is quite limited, and the process involved in obtaining it is partly political.
3. Human beings are viewed as essentially the same across cultures, and are considered to exhibit universal modes of behaviour based upon rationality. However, as Calhoun (1995, p. 77) pointed out 'most claims that that there is a single universal standard of rationality are really claims for the absolute superiority of one standard'.
4. We would accept that some new institutional economists might envisage a recursive relationship between institutions and agents, with the action of agents helping to shape institutional forms. However, we would assert that the third model almost always takes institutions rather than agents as its starting point, and we consider this to be an important weakness.
5. See North (1990, p. 3) where he noted '[i]nstitutions are the rules of the game in a society or, more formally, are the humanly derived constraints that shape human interaction. In consequence they structure incentives in human exchange, whether political, social, or economic. Institutional change shapes the way that societies evolve through time'.
6. As North (1990, p. 5) put it institutions '... evolve and are altered by human beings; hence our theory must begin with the individual. At the same time, the constraints that institutions impose on individual choices are pervasive'.

Chapter 4   Competitive Strategy and Clusters of Innovation

1. See also Chandler 1962, 1977 and Ackroyd and Lawrenson 1996 for contrasting perspectives on this issue.

2. Maskell et al. (1998) point out that while the UK has been much more dependent upon high-tech industries and less dependent on low-tech ones over the past 30 years than the Nordic countries of Sweden, Denmark, Finland, Norway and Iceland, the latter have consistently outperformed the former in terms of GDP per capita, a key indicator of competitiveness.

3. The strategy literature tends to focus on the importance of products, markets and costs, with technology often considered to be a static variable or an operational tool not worthy of inclusion in the overall planning process. Such top down or hierarchical approaches to strategy ignore the dynamic nature of technological change. For many firms, investing in technology allows resources to be capitalised with a view to creating long-term sources of competitive advantage. Agents consider such investments as part of a strategic planning process that helps guard against and negotiate uncertain future conditions, and thus strengthen the long-term viability of their firms.

4. According to Arthur (1992), path dependence is essentially the result of two related and reinforcing processes: positive feedback as represented by increasing returns to scale, and the lock-in process whereby economic agents remain on particular paths of accumulation despite the existence of possible alternatives. In other words, environmental constraints deny agents the inclination or the ability to switch to alternative paths of accumulation or to diversify their potential choices and opportunities.

5. Child (1997, 55) also argued that 'organisational actors do not necessarily, or even typically, deal with an "environment" at arm's length through the impersonal transactions of classical market analysis, but, on the contrary, often engage in relationships with external parties that are sufficiently close and long-standing as to lend a mutually pervasive character to organisation and environment'.

6. Sophisticated forms of this type of alliance are often referred to as heterarchies. According to Grabher (2001, 353–4), heterarchies often contain considerable internal diversity in terms of their organisational forms, ownership structures and philosophies. These are rarely static and are driven by intense rivalry which can lead to the emergence of new and innovative forms of management and organisation. However, these forces of diversity and rivalry are counterbalanced by the practicalities of collaboration. In particular, firms need to develop shared understanding of their circumstances and adopt systems of management and organisation which are compatible if their collaboration is to be productive.

7. Teece makes clear, however, that there are other circumstances in which such arrangements are not suitable.

8. See also Saxenian and Hsu (2001) for an excellent example of collaboration between individuals and firms in Silicon Valley and the Hsinchu-Taipei region of Taiwan.

9. This is based on the assumption that the exchange of goods and services prompts local price and quantity arbitrage adjustments that, over time, push income levels and growth rates towards an equilibrium point in

time and space (Grossman and Helpman 1991, Barro and Sali-I-Martin 1995). It is further assumed that falling transportation costs and increased capital flows, combined with cost differentials encourage greater investment in less developed regions in relation to more developed, higher cost ones (Clark, Feldman and Gertler 2000).

Chapter 5   Cognition, Learning and the New Economy

1. Ackroyd, Glover, Currie and Bull (2000) argue that 'knowledge – and more importantly conceptions of knowledge – are intimately related to particular interests and relations of power' (p. 289). It is the process by which knowledge is constructed and used, rather than the nature of a particular body of knowledge, which influences behaviour.
2. Another, perhaps more profound, reason for supposing that rationality is a spurious characteristic to attribute to agents is that rationality is a cultural conception of meaning which is rooted in the social and economic development of Western society, and the product of a specific set of historical circumstances (Sahlins 1976). In view of this, Lave (1988) argued that 'it is difficult to defend claims for the universality of "rational" modes of good thinking as a scientific yardstick with which to evaluate situated cognitive activities... constructing research in terms of mythological views of scientific thought insures blindness to questions of the structuring of everyday activities themselves' (p. 174).
3. See Klepper (2001) and Adams (2002) for two interesting perspectives on spinoffs.
4. See Huber (1991) for an excellent review of the early literature on organisational learning.
5. Argyris and Schön (1996) are careful to emphasise this point
6. See Martin and Sunley (2003) for a comprehesive critique the cluster concept.
7. See also Maskell (2001)
8. This point is also made by Nonaka and Takeuchi (1995).
9. Antonelli (2000) points out that systems of learning and innovation are 'themselves the – partly – intentional outcome of long-term routines, codes of conduct, and actual investments implemented by the strategic behaviour of agents and governments to increase the innovation capabilities of economic systems... effective connections are the result of deliberate action and should be considered endogenous: an effort has to be made to establish each effective connection' (p. 404). In this chapter we have sought to introduce a cognitive dimension to this process, and to articulate what is distinctive about the patterns of thought and action that characterise innovative behaviour in the IKE.

Bibliography

Ackroyd S., Glover I., Currie W., Bull S. 2000. The triumph of hierarchies over markets: information systems specialists in the current context. In *Professions at Bay: Control and Encouragement of Ingenuity in British Management*, ed. I. Glover, M. Hughes, pp. 263–302. Avebury: Aldershot.

Ackroyd S., Lawrenson D. 1996. Manufacturing decline and the division of labour in Britain. In *The Professional-Managerial Class: Contemporary British Management in the Pursuer Mode*, ed. I. Glover, M. Hughes, pp. 171–193. Aldershot: Avebury.

Adams J.D. 2002. Comparative localization of academic and industrial spillovers. *Journal of Economic Geography* 2: 253–278.

Aldrich H.E. 1979. *Organizations and Environments*. Englewood Cliffs NJ: Prentice-Hall.

Allen F., Gale D. 2000. *Comparing Financial Systems*. Cambridge MA: MIT Press.

Allen J., Massey D., Cochrane A. 1998. *Rethinking the Region*. London: Routledge.

Amin A. 1999. An institutionalist perspective on economic development. *International Journal of Urban and Regional Research* 23: 364–78.

Amin A. 2000. The EU as more than a triad market for national economic spaces. In *The Oxford Handbook of Economic Geography*, ed. G.L. Clark, M.P. Feldman, M.S. Gertler, pp. 671–85. Oxford: Oxford University Press.

Amin A., Thrift N. 1995. Living in the Global. In *Globalisation, Institutions and Regional Development in Europe*, ed. A. Amin, N. Thrift, pp. 1–22. Oxford: Oxford University Press.

Amin A., Tomany J., eds. 1995. *Behind the Myth of the European Union*. London: Routledge.

Antonelli C. 1997. The economics of path-dependence in industrial organisation. *International Journal of Industrial Organisation* 15: 643–75.

Antonelli C. 2000. Restructuring and innovation in long-term regional change. In *The Handbook of Economic Geography*, ed. G.L. Clark, M.P. Feldman, M.S. Gertler, pp. 395–410. Oxford: Oxford University Press.

Antonelli C. 2001. *The Microeconomics of Technological Change*. Oxford: Oxford University Press.

Archer M.S., 1996. *Culture and Agency: The Place of Culture in Social Theory*. Cambridge: Cambridge University Press.

Archer M.S., 2000. *Being Human: The Problem of Agency*. Cambridge: Cambridge University Press.

Argyris C. 1990. *Overcoming Organisational Defences*. Boston: Allyn and Bacon.

Argyris C., Schön D.A. 1978. *Organizational Learning: A Theory of Action Perspective*. Reading, MA: Addison-Wesley.

Argyris C., Schön D.A. 1996. *Organizational Learning II: Theory, Method and Practice*. Reading, MA: Addison-Wesley.

Armstrong H. 2001. Regional selective assistance: is the spend enough and is it targeting the right places. *Regional Studies* 35: 247–58.

Armstrong H., Kehrer B., Wells P. 2001. The initial impacts of community economic development initiatives in the Yorkshire and Humber structural funds programme. *Regional Studies* 25: 247–58.

Armstrong H., Taylor J. 2000. *Regional Economics and Policy*. Oxford: Blackwell.

Arthur W.B. 1990. Positve feedbacks in the economy. *Scientific American* 262: 80–5.

Arthur W.B. 1994. *Increasing Returns and Path Dependence in the Economy*. Ann Arbor: University of Michigan Press.

Asheim B.T. 1996. Industrial districts as 'learning regions': a condition for prosperity? *European Planning Studies* 4: 379–400.

Asheim B.T. 2000. Industrial districts: the contributions of Marshall and beyond. In *The Oxford Handbook of Economic Geography*, ed. G.L. Clark, M. Feldman, M.S. Gertler, pp. 413–31. Oxford: Oxford University Press.

Barnes, T.J. 1994. Probable writing: derrida, deconstruction and the quantitative revolution in human geography. *Environment and Planning A* 26: 1021–1040.

Barrie R., Jukes R. 2001. UK economics: trading places. Discussion paper. Credit Suisse First Boston (Europe).

Barro R., Sala-I-Martin X. 1995. *Economic Growth*. New York: McGraw-Hill.

Bateson G. 1972. *Steps to an Ecology of Mind*. San Francisco: Chandler Publishing Company.

Bathelt H. 2001. The rise of a new cultural products industry cluster in Germany: the case of the Leipzig media industry. Department of Economic and Social Geography Working Paper (06-2001). Johann Wolfgang Goethe-Universität, Frankfurt.

Bathelt H. 2002. The re-emergence of a media industry cluster in Leipzig. *European Planning Studies* 10, 583–611.

Bathelt H., Glückler J. 2000. Netzerke, lernen und evolutionaare regionalentwicklung. *Zeitschrift fur Wirtschaftsgeographie* 44: 167–82.

Bathelt H., Glückler J. 2003. Toward a relational economic geography. *Journal of Economic Geography* 3, 117–144.

Bathelt H., Malmberg A., Maskell P. 2002. Clusters and local knowledge: local buzz, global pipelines and the process of knowledge creation. Working Paper 02-12, Danish Research Unit for Industrial Dynamics.

Bebchuk L., Roe M.J. 1999. A theory of path dependence in corporate ownership and governance. *Stanford Law Review* 52: 127–70.

Beckert J. 1999. Agency, entrepreneurs, and institutional change. The role of strategic choice and institutionalised practices in organizations. *Organization Studies* 20: 777–99.

Bicchieri C. 1993. *Rationality and Coordination*. Cambridge: Cambridge University Press.

Blackler F. 1995. Knowledge work and organization: an overview and interpretation. *Organization Studies* 16: 1021–46.

Boland R.J., Tenaki R.V. 1995. Perspective making and perspective taking in communities of knowing. *Organization Science* 6: 350–372.

Bonvicini G. 2000. Comments on S. Arzeni 'Local and regional governance and globalisation: logic, trends and challenges in Europe'. In *Global Governance, Regionalism and the International Economy*, ed. P. Guerrieri, H-E. Scharrer, pp. 277–80. Baden-Baden: Nomos Verlagsgesellscahft in conjunction with IAI.

Bratman M.E. 1987. *Intention, Plans, Practical Reason*. Cambridge MA: Harvard University Press.

Braun E., Polt W. 1988. High technology and competitiveness: An Austrian perspective. In *Small Countries Facing the Technological Revolution*, ed. C. Freeman, B. Lundvall, pp. 203–225. London: Pinter.

Breschi S., Malerba F. 1997. Sectorial innovation systems: technological regimes, Schumpeterian dynamics and spatial boundaries. In *Systems of Innovation: Technologies, Institutions and Organisations*, ed. C. Edquist, pp. 130–56. London: Pinter.

Bresnahan T., Gambardella A., Saxenian A. 2001. 'Old Economy' inputs for 'New Economy' outcomes: cluster formation in the new Silicon Valleys. *Industrial and Corporate Change* 10: 835–860.

Brons M., de Groot H.L.F., Nijkamp P. 2000. Growth effects in government policies: A comparative multi-country context. *Growth and Change* 31: 547–72.

Burt R.S. 1992. *Structural Holes: The Social Structure of Competition*. Cambridge, MA: Harvard University Press.

Calhoun C. 1995. *Critical Social Theory*. Oxford: Blackwell.

Carter S. 1996. Small business marketing. In *International Encyclopedia of Business and Management*, ed M. Warner, pp. 4502–4509. London: Routledge.

Castells M. 1996. *The Rise of the Network Society*. Malden, MA: Blackwell.

Castells M., Hall P.G. 1994. *Technopoles of the World: The Makings of 21st Century Industrial Complexes*. London: Routledge.

Chandler A.D. 1962. *Strategy and Structure: Chapters in the History of Industrial Enterprise*. Cambridge MA: Harvard University Press.

Chandler A.D. 1977. *The Visible Hand: The Managerial Revolution in American Business*. Cambridge MA: Harvard University Press.

Charles D. 2002. The evolution of European science and technology policy and its links to the cohesion agenda. In *Regulation of Science and Technology Policy*, ed. H. Lawton Smith, pp. 97–126. Basingstoke: Palgrave.

Child J. 1972. Organization structure, environment and performance. The role of strategic choice. *Sociology* 6: 1–22.

Child J. 1996. Strategic choice. In *International Encyclopedia of Business and Management*, ed. M Warner, pp. 4556–71. London: Routledge.

Child J. 1997. Strategic choice in the analysis of action, structure, organizations and environment: Retrospect and Prospect. *Organization Studies* 18: 43–76.

Child J., Faulkner D. 1998. *Strategies of Cooperation: Managing Alliances, Networks and Joint Ventures*. Oxford: Oxford University Press.

Clark G.L. 1993. Global interdependence and regional development: business linkages and corporate governance in a world of financial risk. *Transactions, Institute of British Geographers* NS 18: 309–25.

Clark G.L. 1994. Strategy and structure: corporate restructuring and the scope and characteristics of sunk costs. *Environment and Planning A* 26: 9–32.

Clark G.L. 1998. Stylised facts and close dialogue: methodology in economic geography. *Annals, Association of American Geographers* 88: 74–89.

Clark G.L. 2000. *Pension Fund Capitalism*. Oxford: Oxford University Press.

Clark G.L. 2001. Code words for the new millennium: the vocabulary of Europe. *Society and Space* 19: 697–717.

Clark G.L. 2003. *European Pensions and Global Finance*. Oxford: Oxford University Press.

Clark G.L., Feldman M., Gertler M.S. 2000a. Economic geography: transition and growth. In *The Oxford Handbook of Economic Geography*, ed. G.L. Clark, M. Feldman, M.S. Gertler, pp. 3–17. Oxford: Oxford University Press.

Clark G.L. Feldman M. Gertler M.S. 2000b. *The Oxford Handbook of Economic Geography*, ed. G.L. Clark, M. Feldman, M.S. Gertler. Oxford: Oxford University Press.

Clark G.L., Feldman M., Gertler M.S. eds. 2001. *The Oxford Handbook of Economic Geography*. Oxford: Oxford University Press.

Clark G.L., Gertler M.S., Whiteman J. 1986. *Regional Dynamics: Studies in Adjustment Theory*. London: Allen and Unwin.

Clark G.L., Kim W.B. eds. 1995. *Asian NIEs in the Global Economy*. Baltimore: Johns Hopkins University Press.

Clark G.L., Mansfield D., Tickell A. 2001. Emergent frameworks in global finance. *Economic Geography* 77: 250–271.

Clark G.L., Mansfield D., Tickell A. 2002. Global finance and the German model: German corporations, market incentives, and the management of employer-sponsored pension institutions. *Transactions of the Institute of British Geographers* 27: 91–110.

Clark G.L., Marshall J.C. 2002. Decision-making: models of the real-world and expertise. Paper presented at the National Association of Pension Funds Conference, Edinburgh, March 2002.

Clark G.L., Wrigley N. 1997. Exit, the firm and sunk costs: re-conceptualising the corporate geography of disinvestments and plant closure. *Progress in Human Geography* 21: 338–58.

Coleman J. 1990. *Foundations of Social Theory*. Cambridge MA: Harvard University Press.

Cooke P. 2001. Regional innovation systems, clusters and the knowledge economy. *Industrial and Corporate Change* 10: 945–974.

Cooke P., Morgan K. 1998. The Associational Economy: Firms, Regions and Innovation. Oxford: Oxford University Press.

Cowie F. 1999. *What's Within? Nativism Reconsidered*. Oxford: Oxford University Press.

Crouch C., Streeck W. 1997. Introduction: The future of capitalist diversity. In *Political Economy of Modern Capitalism. Mapping Convergence and Diversity*, ed. C. Crouch, W. Streeck, pp. 1–18. London: Sage.

Crouch C., Streeck W., eds. 1997. Political Economy of Modern Capitalism. Mapping Convergence and Diversity. London: Sage.

Curry L. 1998. *The Random Spatial Economy and Its Evolution*. Basingstoke: Ashgate Publishing Company.

Cyert R.M., March J.G. 1992. *A Behavioural Theory of the Firm*. Cambridge MA: Blackwell.

David P. 1985. Clio and the economics of QWERTY. *American Economic Review* 75: 332–7.

Dicken P. 1992. Global Shift: The Internationalization of Economic Activity. London: Paul Chapman (2nd Edition).

Dicken P. 1999. Globalisation – An economic-geographical perspective. In *21st Century Economics: Perspectives of Socioeconomics for a Changing World*, ed. W.E. Halal, K.B. Taylor, pp. 31–51. Basingstoke: MacMillan.

Dicken P. 2000. Places and flows: situating international investment. In *The Oxford Handbook of Economic Geography*, ed. G.L. Clark, M. Feldman, M.S. Gertler, pp. 275–91. Oxford: Oxford University Press.

Dierkes M., Wagner P. 1992. European and social science in transition: conclusions and recommendations. In *European Social Science in Transition: Assessment and Outlook*, ed. M. Dierkes, P. Wagner, pp. 611–37. Boulder: Westview Press.

Diez M.A. 2001. The evaluation of regional innovation and cluster policies: towards a participatory approach. *European Planning Studies* 9: 907–23.

Dore R. 2000. *Stock Market Capitalism: Welfare Capitalism. Japan and Germany versus the Anglo Saxons*. Oxford: Oxford University Press.

Dosi G. 1988. Institutions and markets in a dynamic world. *The Manchester School* 56: 119–46.

Drummond H. 1996. *Escalation of Decision-Making*. Oxford: Oxford University Press.

Dunford M., Perrons D. 1983. *The Arena of Capital*. London: Macmillan.

Dunning J. 1997. *Alliance Capitalism and Global Business*. London: Routledge.

Dunning J.H. 1998. Globalization, technological change and the spatial organization of economic activity. In *The Dynamic Firm*, ed. A.D. Chandler, P. Hagström, O. Sölvell, pp. 289–314. Oxford: Oxford University Press.

Dunning J.H. 1999. Regions, globalization and the knowledge economy: the issues stated. In *Regions, Globalization and the Knowledge-Based Economy*, ed. J.H. Dunning, pp. 7–41. Oxford: Oxford University Press.

Ernst D. 2001. Small firms competing in globalised high-tech industries: the co-evolution of domestic and international knowledge linkages in Taiwan's computer industry. In *The Global Challenge to Industrial Districts: Small and Medium Sized Enterprises in Italy and Taiwan*, eds. P. Guerrieri, S. Iammarino and C. Pietrobelli, pp. 95–130. Cheltenham: Edward Elgar.

European Commission. 1994. The European Report on Science and Technology Indicators 1994. Luxembourg: EC EUR 15897 EN.

European Commission. 1999. *XXVIIIth Report on Competition Policy 1998*, Official Publications of the European Communities, Luxembourg.

European Commission. 2000. Real convergence and catching up in the EU. In *The EU Economy: 2000 Review*, ed. European Commission, pp. 175–206. Luxembourg: Office for Official Publications of the European Communities (European Economy No. 71).

Feldman M.P. 1994. *The Geography of Innovation*. Boston: Kluwer Academic Publishers.

Feldman M. 2001. The entrepreneurial event revisited: firm formation in a regional context. *Industrial and Corporate Change* 10: 861–891.

Florida R. 2002. Bohemia and economic geography. *Journal of Economic Geography* 2: 55–71.

Foray D. 1997. The dynamic implications of increasing returns: technological change and path inefficiency. *International Journal of Industrial Organization* 15: 733–52.

Fujimoto T. 1999. The Evolution of a Manufacturing System at Toyota. Oxford: Oxford University Press.

Gambarotto F., Maggioni M.A. 1998. Regional development strategies in changing environments: An ecological approach. *Regional Studies* 32: 49–61.

Geertz C. 1974. *The Interpretation of Cultures*. London: Hutchinson.

Gertler M.S. 2001. Best Practice? Geography, learning and the institutional limits to strong convergence. *Journal of Economic Geography* 1: 5–26.

Gertler M.S. 2002. Tacit knowledge and the economic geography of context OR the undefinable tacitness of being (there). Mimeo. Toronto: Munk Centre for International Studies, University of Toronto.

Gertler M.S. 2003. A cultural economic geography of production: are we learning by doing? In *The Handbook of Cultural Geography*, ed. K. Anderson, M. Domoshm, S. Pile, N. Thrift, pp. 131–146. London: Sage.

Gibbs D.C., Jonas A.E.G., Reimer S., Spooner D.J. 2001. Governance, institutional capacity and partnership in local economic development: theoretical issues and empirical evidence from the Humber Sub-region. *Transactions of the Institute of British Geographers* 26: 103–19.

Gibson J., Graham K. 1997. *The End of Capitalism (As We Knew It)*. Oxford: Blackwell.

Giddens A. 1986. *The Constitution of Society: Outline of the Theory of Structuration*. Cambridge: Polity Press.

Giddens A. 1987. *Social Theory and Modern Sociology*. Cambridge: Polity.

Gigerenzer G. 2001. The adaptive toolbox. In *Bounded Rationality: The Adaptive Toolbox*, ed. G. Gigerenzer, R. Selten, pp. 37–50. Cambridge MA: MIT Press.

Gigerenzer G., Selten R. 2001. Rethinking rationality. In *Bounded Rationality: The adaptive toolbox*, ed. G. Gigerenzer, R. Selten, pp. 1–12. Cambridge MA: MIT Press.

Gigerenzer G., Todd P. 1999. *Simple Heuristics that Make Us Smart*. Oxford: Oxford University Press.

Grabher G. 1993. *The Embedded Firm: On the Socio-Economics of Industrial Networks*. London: Routledge.

Grabher G. 2001. Ecologies of creativity: the village, the group and the heterarchic organisation of the British advertising industry. *Environment and Planning A* 33: 351–374.

Grande E. 2001. Institutions and interest: interest groups in the European system of multi-level governance. Munchen: Lehstuhl fur Politicshe Wissenschaft Tecnicje Universitat Munchen Working Paper No. 1.

Grande E., Peschke A. 1999. Transnational cooperation and policy networks in European science policy-making. *Research Policy* 28: 43–61.

Granovetter M. 1973. The strength of weak ties. *American Journal of Sociology* 78: 1360–1380.

Granovetter M. 1985. Economic action and economic structure. The problem of embeddedness. *American Journal of Sociology* 91: 481–510.

Grossman G., Helpman E. 1991. *Innovation and Growth in the Global Economy*. Cambridge, MA: MIT Press.

Guerrieri P., Scharrer H-E., eds. 2000. *Global Governance, Regionalism and the International Economy*. Baden-Baden: Nomos Verlagsgesellschaft in conjunction with IAI.

Hall E.T., Hall M.R. 1990. *Understanding Cultural Differences*. Yarmouth MA: Intercultural Press.

Hall P.A., Soskice D. 2001. *Varieties of Capitalism: The Institutional Foundations of Comparative Advantage*. Oxford: Oxford University Press.

Hall W. 1995. *Managing Cultures: Making Strategic Relationships Work*. Chichester: Wiley.

Hannan M.T., Freeman J. 1989. *Organizational Ecology*. Cambridge MA: Harvard University Press.

Hasselbadh H., Kallinikos J. 2000. The project of rationalization: a critique and reappraisal of neo-institutionalism in organization studies. *Organization Studies* 21: 697–720.

Healy K. 1988. Conceptualising constraint: Mouzelis, Archer and the concept of social structure. *Sociology* 32: 509–522.

Henderson D. 2000. EU regional innovation strategies: regional experimentation in practice? *European Urban and Regional Studies* 7: 347–58.

Hirst P. 1994. *Associative Democracy: New Forms of Social Governance*. Cambridge: Polity.

Hodgson G.M. 1996. Institutional Economics. In *International Encyclopedia of Business and Management*, ed. M Warner, pp. 2174–89. London: Routledge.

Hoffman L.F., Maier N.R.F. 1961. Quality and acceptance of problem solutions by members homogenous and heterogeneous groups. *Journal of Abnormal and Social Psychology* 62: 401–407.

Hofstede G. 1980. *Culture's Consequences: International Differences in Work-Related Values*. Beverly Hills CA: Sage.

Hofstede G. 1991. *Cultures and Organizations*. Maidenhead: McGraw-Hill.

Hollingsworth J.R., Boyer R., eds. 1997. *Contemporary Capitalism: The Embeddedness of Institutions*. Cambridge: Cambridge University Press.

Hollis M. 1996. *Reason in Action: Essays in the Philosophy of Social Science*. Cambridge: Cambridge University Press.

Hotz-Hart B. 2000. Innovation networks, regions and globalization. In *The Oxford Handbook of Economic Geography*, ed. G.L. Clark, M.P. Feldman, M.S. Gertler, pp. 432–450. Oxford: Oxford University Press.

Huber G.P. 1991. Organizational learning: the contributing processes and the literatures. *Organization Science* 2: 88–115.

Huggins R. 1996. Technology policy, networks and small firms in Denmark. *Regional Studies* 30: 523–6.

Huggins R. 1998. Local business co-operation and training and enterprise councils: The development of inter-firm networks. *Regional Studies* 32: 813–26.

Husband J., Gerrard B. 2001. Formal aid in an informal sector: institutional support for ethnic minority enterprise in local clothing and textile industries. *Journal of Ethnic and Migration Studies* 27: 115–31.

Janis I.L. 1982. *Groupthink: Psychological Studies of Policy Decision and Fiascos.* Boston: Houghton Mifflin (2nd Edition).

Jensen M.C. 1998. *Foundations of Organizational Strategy.* Cambridge MA: Harvard University Press.

Jessop B. 2001. Institutional re(turns) and the strategic-relational approach. *Environment and Planning A* 33: 1213–1235.

Jones M. 2001. The rise of the regional state in economic governance. *Environment and Planning* 33: 1185–212.

Kahneman D., Tversky A. 1986. Rational choice and the framing of decisions. *Journal of Business* 59: 250–78.

Kaldor N. 1970. The case for regional policies. *Scottish Journal of Political Economy* 17: 337–48.

Kaufman A., Todtling F. 2000. Systems of innovation in transitional industrial regions: the case of Syria in a comparative perspective. *Regional Studies* 34: 29–40.

Keeble D., Wilkinson F. 1999. Collective learning and knowledge development in the evolution of regional clusters of high technology SMEs in Europe. *Regional Studies* 33: 295–303.

Kern H. 1996. Vertrauensverlust und blindes Vertrauen. Intergrationsprobleme inn ökonomischen Handeln. *SOFI-Mitteilungen* 24: 7–14.

Keynes J.M. 1921. *A Treatise on Probability.* London: Macmillan.

Klepper S. 2001. Employee startups in high-tech industries. *Industrial and Corporate Change* 10: 639–674.

Knight F. 1921. *Risk, Uncertainty and Profit.* New York: Houghton Mifflin.

Kreps D.M. 1990. *Game Theory and Economic Modelling.* Oxford: Oxford University Press.

Krugman P. 1991. *Geography and Trade.* Cambridge MA: MIT Press.

Lakoff G., Johnson M. 1980. *Metaphors We Live By.* Chicago: University of Chicago Press.

Lam A. 1997. Embedded firms, embedded knowledge: problems of collaboration and knowledge transfer in global cooperative ventures. *Organizational Studies* 18, 973–996.

Laurent A. 1983. The cultural diversity of Western conceptions of management. *International Studies of Management and Organization* 13: 75–96.

Laurent A. 1986. The cross-cultural puzzle of international human resource management. *Human Resource Management* 25: 91–102.

Lave J. 1988. *Cognition in Practice: Mind Mathematics and Culture in Everyday Life.* Cambridge: Cambridge University Press.

Lawton Smith H. 2001. Promoting local growth in the Oxfordshire high-tech economy: local institutional settings. In *Promoting Local Growth: Process,*

Practice and Policy, eds. D. Felsenstein, M. Taylor, pp. 117 163. Aldershot: Ashgate.

Lazerson M.H., Lorenzoni G. 1999. The firms that feed industrial districts: A return to the Italian source. *Industrial and Corporate Change* 8: 235-266.

Le Heron R., McDermott P. 2001. Rethinking Auckland: local responses to global challenges. In *Promoting Local Growth, Process, Practice and Policy*, ed. D. Felsenstein, M. Taylor, pp. 365-386. London: Ashgate.

Leeds C., Kirkbride P.S., Duncan J. 1994. The cultural context of Europe. In *Human Resource Management in Europe*, ed. P.S. Kirkbride, pp. 11-27. London: Routledge.

Levitt B., March J.G. 1988. Organisational learning. *Annual Review of Sociology* 14: 319-40.

Lindblom C. 1959. The science of muddling through. *Public Administration Review* 19: 79-88.

Lindblom C. 1965. *The Intelligence of Democracy: Decision-Making Through Mutual Adjustment*. New York: The Free Press.

Lipset S.M. 1963. *The First New Nation: The United States in Historical and Comparative Perspective*. New York: Basic Books.

Lipset S.M. 1986. Historical traditions and national characteristics – a comparative analysis of Canada and the United States. *Canadian Journal of Sociology* 11: 113-55.

Lipset S.M. 1990. *Continental Divide: The Values and Institutions of the US and Canada*. New York: Routledge.

Lovering J. 2001. The coming regional crisis (And how to avoid it). *Regional Studies* 35: 349-54.

Lundvall B-Å., ed. 1992. *National Systems of Innovation: Towards a Theory of Innovation and Interactive Learning*. London: Pinter.

McKendrick D.G., Doner R.F., Haggard S. 2000. *From Silicon Valley to Singapore: Location and Competitive Advantage in the Hard Disk Drive Industry*. Stanford: Stanford University Press.

McKinlay A., Zeitlin J. 1986. The meanings of organizational prerogative: industrial relations and the organization of work in British engineering, 1880-1939. *Business History* 31, 32-47.

Macharzina K., Brodel D. 1996. Strategy and technological development. In *International Encyclopedia of Business and Management*, ed. M. Warner, pp. 4691-4701. London: Routledge.

Malecki E.J., Maskell P. 2001. The R&D location of the firm and creative regions: a survey. *Technovation* 6: 205-22.

Malmberg A. 1997. Industrial geography, location and learning. *Progress in Human Geography* 21: 573-582.

Malmberg A., Maskell P. 2001. The elusive concept of localization economies: towards a knowledge-based theory of spatial clustering. Paper presented at the Association of American Geographers Annual Conference, New York, February/March 2001.

March J.G. 1981. Decision-making in perspective: decisions in organisations and theories of choice. In *Perspectives on Organisation Design and Behaviour*, ed. A. Van de Ven, W. Joyce, pp. 205-44. New York: John Wiley.

March J.G. 1994. *A Primer of Decision-Making: How Decisions Happen.* New York: Free Press.

March J.G., Simon H.A. 1958. *Organizations.* New York: John Wiley.

Marshall A. 1890. *Principles of Economics.* London: Macmillan.

Martin R. 2001. EM versus the regions? Regional convergence and divergence in Euroland. *Journal of Economic Geography* 1: 51–80.

Martin R., Sunley P. 2003. Deconstructing clusters: chaotic concept or policy panacea? *Journal of Economic Geography* 3, 5–35.

Maskell P. 2001. Towards a knowledge-based theory of the geographical cluster. *Industrial and Corporate Change* 10: 921–943.

Maskell P., Eskelinen H., Hannibalsson I., Malmberg A., Vatne E. 1998. *Competitiveness, Localised Learning and Regional Development.* London: Routledge.

Mayntz R. 1993. Modernization and the logic of interorganizational networks. In *Societal Change Between Market and Organization*, eds. J. Child, M. Crozier, R. Mayntz, pp. 3–18. Aldershot: Avebury.

Meiksins P., Smith C. 1996. *Engineering Labour.* London: Verso.

Monti M. 1996. *The Single Market and Tomorrow's Europe.* London: Kogan Page.

Morgan G. 1997. *Images of Organization.* Thousand Oaks CA: Sage.

Morgan K., Nauwelaers C. 1999. *Regional Innovation Strategies: The Challenge for the Less-Favoured Regions.* London: The Stationery Office.

Moss Kanter R., Corn R.I. 1994. Do cultural differences make a business difference? Contextual factors affecting cross-cultural relationship success. *The Journal of Management Development* 13: 5–23.

Moulaert F. 2000. *Globalisation and Integrated Area Development in European Cities.* Oxford: Oxford University Press.

Mouzelis N. 1995. *Sociological Theory: What Went Wrong?* New York: Routledge.

Nelson R., Sampat B.N. 1998. *Making Sense of Institutions as a Factor Shaping Economic Performance.* Columbia University New York: Mimeo.

Nelson R.R., Winter S.G. 1982. *An Evolutionary Theory of Economic Change.* Cambridge, MA: Harvard University Press.

New C. 1994. Structure, agency and social transformation. *Journal for the Theory of Social Behaviour* 24: 187–205.

Nonaka I., Takeuchi H. 1995. *The Knowledge-Creating Company: How Japanese Companies Create the Dynamics of Innovation.* Oxford: Oxford University Press.

North D. 1990. *Institutions, Institutional Change and Economic Performance.* Cambridge: Cambridge University Press.

Nooteboom B. 2000. *Learning and Innovation in Organizations and Economies.* Oxford: Oxford University Press.

Nooteboom B. 2001. Problems and solutions in knowledge transfer. Paper presented at Max Planck Institute Conference on the influence of co-operation, networks and institutions on regional innovation systems, Jena, February 2001.

Nooteboon B. 2002. A cognitive theory of the firm. Paper presented at a workshop on theories of the firm, Paris, November 2002.

O'Sullivan M., Giangrande M. 2002. Is Ireland a muse or a mystic for regional development? Working Paper 02 21. Oxford: University of Oxford.

Owen-Smith J., Riccaboni M., Pammolli F., Powell W.W. 2002. A comparison of US and European university-industry relations in the life sciences. *Management Science* 48: 24–43.

Ozawa T. 1999. Organizational efficiency and structural change: a meso-level analysis. In *Structural Change and Cooperation in the Global Economy*, ed. G. Boyd, J.H. Dunning, pp. 160–190. Cheltenham: Edward Elgar.

Paasi A. 2001. Europe as a social process and discourse: considerations of place, boundaries and identity. *European Urban and Regional Studies* 8: 7–28.

Painter J. 2001. Space, Territory and the European Project: Reflections on Agnew and Paasi. *European Urban and Regional Studies* 8: 42–3.

Panopoulou M. 2001. Corporate investment and information technologies: the case of the Greek refining industry. *Technology Analysis and Strategic Management* 13: 281–303.

Peck F., McGuinness D. 2001. UK competitiveness and the regional agenda: making sense of clusters in the north of England. Paper presented at Regional Studies Association European Conference, Gdansk, September 2001.

Pelkmans J. 2001. European integration, economic and institutional convergence. In *Global Governance, Regionalism and the International Economy*, ed. P. Guerrieri, H-E. Scharrer, pp. 37–86. Baden-Baden: Nomos Verlagsgesellescahft in conjunction with IAI.

Penrose E.T. 1952. Biological analogies in the theory of the firm. *American Economic Review* 42: 804–19.

Perry M. 1996. Network intermediaries and their effectiveness. *International Small Business Journal* 14: 72–80.

Piore M., Sabel C.F. 1984. *The Second Industrial Divide: Possibilities for Prosperity*. New York: Basic Books.

Polanyi K. 1996. *The Tacit Dimension*. London: Routledge & Kegan Paul.

Porter M.E. 1990. *The Competitive Advantages of Nations*. New York: The Free Press.

Porter M.E. 1998. *Competitive Advantage: Creating and Sustaining Superior Performance*. New York: The Free Press.

Porter M.E. 2000. Locations, clusters, and company strategy. In *The Oxford Handbook of Economic Geography*, ed. G.L. Clark, M. Feldman, M.S. Gertler, pp. 253–274. Oxford: Oxford University Press.

Radner R., Stiglitz J. 1984. A non-concavity in the value of information. In *Bayesian Models in Economic Theory*, ed. M. Boyer, R.E. Kihlstrom, pp. 378–97. Amsterdam: Elsevier.

Reich R. 1990. But now we're global. *The Times Literary Supplement* August 31–September 6: 925–926.

Reinert E.S. 1995. Competitiveness and its predecessors – a 500-year cross national perspective. *Structural Change and Economic Dynamics* 6: 23–42.

Rex J. 1974. *Sociology and the Demystification of the Modern World*. London: Routledge and Keegan Paul.

Reynolds P.D. 1999. New and small firms in expanding markets. In *Small and Medium-sized Enterprises in the Global Economy*, ed. Z.J. Acs, B. Yeung, pp. 15–23. Ann Arbor: University of Michigan Press.

Roe M.J. 2000. Political preconditions to separating ownership from corporate control. *Stanford Law Review* 53: 539–606.

Romijn H., Albaladejo M. 2000. Country Study of the United Kingdom. Report for TSE SMEs in Europe and East Asia: Competition, collaboration and lessons for policy support, Queen Elizabeth House, Oxford.

Sabel C. 1995. Conclusion: turning the page in industrial districts. In *Small and Medium-Sized Enterprises*, ed. A. Bagnasco and C. Sabel, pp. 134–158. London: Pinter.

Sahlins M.D. 1976. *Culture and Practical Reason*. Chicago: Chicago University Press.

Said E. 1978. *Orientalism*. Cambridge MA: Harvard University Press.

Sanchez. 2001. The Design of European Innovation Policy: Issues and Problems. Paper prepared as part of the project 'Innovation Policy in a Knowledge based Economy'. Commissioned by the European Commission. Mimeo Autonomous, University of Madrid.

Saxenian A. 1994. *Regional Advantage: Culture and Competition in Silicon Valley and Route 128*. Cambridge MA: Harvard University Press.

Saxenian A., Hsu J. 2001. The Silicon Valley-Hsinchu connection: technical communities and industrial upgrading. *Industrial and Corporate Change* 10: 893–920.

Sayer A. 1992. (2nd edition) *Method in Social Science: A Realist Approach*. London: Routledge.

Scharpf F.W. 1993. Coordination in hierarchies and networks. In *Games in Hierarchies and Networks: Analytical and Empirical Approaches to the Study of Governance Institutions*, ed. F.W. Scharpf, pp. 125–165. Boulder Colorado: Westview Press.

Schumpeter J.A. 1942. *Capitalism, Socialism and Democracy*. New York: Harper.

Scott A.J. 1998. *Regions and the World Economy: The Coming Shape of Global Production, Competition, and Political Order*. Oxford: Oxford University Press.

Scott A. 2000. Economic geography: the great half-century. In *The Oxford Handbook of Economic Geography*, ed. G.L. Clark, M. Feldman, M.S. Gertler, pp. 18–44. Oxford: Oxford University Press.

Scott B., Lodge G. eds. 1985. *US Competitiveness and the World Economy*. Boston, MA: Harvard Business School Press.

Sedgwick P. 1999. Rationality. In *Key Concepts in Cultural Theory*, eds. A. Edgar, P. Sedgwick, pp. 326–329. London: Routledge.

Senge P. 1992. *The Fifth Discipline: The Art and Practice of the Learning Organization*. London: Century Business.

Sewell W.H. 1992. A theory of structure: duality, agency and transformation. *American Journal of Sociology* 98: 1–29.

Shiller R. 2000. *Irrational Exuberance*. Princeton: Princeton University Press.

Shleifer A. 2000. *Inefficient Markets: An Introduction to Behavioral Finance*. Oxford: Oxford University Press.

Silverman D. 1970. *The Theory of Organisations*. London: Heinemann.

Simon H. 1955. A behavioural model of rational choice. *Quarterly Journal of Economics* 69: 99–118.

Simon H. 1956. Rational choice and the structure of environments. *Psychology Review* 63: 129–38.

Simon H. 1986. Rationality in psychology and economics. *The Journal of Business* 59: S209–S24.

Simon H. 1987. Bounded rationality. In *The New Palgrave Dictionary of Economics*, eds. J. Eatwell, M. Milgate, P. Newman, pp. 266–268. London: Macmillan.

Simon H. 1997. Models of Bounded Rationality: Empirically Grounded Reason. Cambridge MA: MIT Press.

Smith A. 1776. *The Wealth of Nations*. London: Dent.

Smith A. 2001. Going global, going local: power relations, industrial clusters and regional transformations in the East European Clothing Industry. Presented at Regional Studies Association Conference on Regional Transitions, Gdansk, Poland.

Smith K. 2000. What is the knowledge economy? Knowledge-intensive industries and distributed knowledge bases. Paper prepared as part of the 'Innovation Policy in a Knowledge-Based Economy'. Oslo, Norway: European Commission STEP Group.

Spence M. 1981. The learning curve and competition. *Bell Journal of Economics* 12: 49–70.

Steiner G. 1995. What is comparative literature? Inaugural Lecture, University of Oxford. Oxford: Clarendon Press.

Steinmo S., Tolbert C.J. 1998. Do institutions really matter? Taxation in industrialised democracies. *Comparative Political Studies* 31: 65–87.

Stigler G. 1961. The economics of information. *Journal of Political Economy* 69: 213–25.

Storper M. 1995. The resurgence of regional economies, ten years later: the region as a nexus of untraded interdependencies. *European Urban and Regional Studies* 2: 191–221.

Storper M. 1997. *The Regional World: Territorial Development in a Global Economy*. New York: The Guildford Press.

Storper M. 2000. Globalization, localization and trade. In *The Oxford Handbook of Economic Geography*, ed. G.L. Clark, M.P. Feldman, M.S. Gertler, pp. 146–165. Oxford: Oxford University Press.

Storper M., Salais R. 1997. *Worlds of Production. The Action Frameworks of the Economy*. Cambridge MA: Harvard University Press.

Strange S. 1997. The future of global capitalism; or will divergence persist forever? In *Political Economy of Modern Capitalism. Mapping Convergence and Diversity*, ed. C. Crouch, W. Streeck, pp. 182–91. London: Sage.

Streeck W. 1997. German capitalism: does it exist? Can it survive? In *Political Economy of Modern Capitalism. Mapping Convergence and Diversity*, ed. C. Crouch, W. Streeck, pp. 33–54. London: Sage.

Swyngedouw E. 2000. Elite power, global forces, and the political economy of 'glocal' development. In *The Oxford Handbook of Economic Geography*, ed. G.L. Clark, M. Feldman, M.S. Gertler, pp. 541–58. Oxford: Oxford University Press.

Swyngedouw E., Baeten G. 2001. Scaling the city: the political economy of 'glocal' development – Brussels' conundrum. *European Planning Studies* 9: 827–49.

Taylor M.J., Thrift N.J. 1982. Models of corporate development and the multinational corporation. In *The Geography of Multinationals*, ed. M.J. Taylor, N.J. Thrift, pp. 14–32. New York: St Martin's Press.

Teece D.J. 1992. Competition, cooperation and innovation: organizational arrangements for regimes of rapid technological progress. *Journal of Economic Behaviour and Organization* 18:1–25.

Teece D.J. 2000. *Managing Intellectual Capital: Organizational, Strategic and Policy Dimensions*. Oxford: Oxford University Press.

Thaler R. 1994. *Quasi-Rational Economics*. New York: Russell Sage Foundation.

Thompson J.D. 1998. *Organizations in Action*. New York: McGraw-Hill.

Thrift N. 2000. Pandora's box: cultural geographies of economies. In *The Oxford Handbook of Economic Geography*, ed. G.L. Clark, M. Feldman, M.S. Gertler, pp. 689–704. Oxford: Oxford University Press.

Tracey P., Clark G.L., Lawton Smith H. 2001. On the margin: the performance of UK SMEs in labour intensive industries. Working Paper 01–16. Oxford: University of Oxford.

Triandis H.C., Hall E.R., Ewen R.B. 1965. Member heterogeneity and dyadic creativity. *Human Relations* 18: 33–55.

Trompenaars F. 1988. *The Organisation of Meaning and the Meaning of Organisation*. Modified version of doctoral thesis thesis. University of Pennsylvania, Philadelphia.

Trompenaars F. 1997. *Riding the Waves of Culture: Understanding Cultural Diversity in Business*. London: Nicholas Brealey (2nd Edition).

Van Witteloostuijn A. 1996. Contexts and environments. In *International Encylopaedia of Business and Management*, ed. M Warner, pp. 752–761. London: Routledge.

Waters R., Lawton Smith H. 2002. RDAs and local economic development: scale and competitiveness in Oxfordshire and Cambridgeshire. *European Planning Studies* 10: 633–649.

Weick K.E. 1979. *The Social Psychology of Organizing*. Reading MA: Addison-Wesley.

Wiener J. 1999. *Globalization and the Harmonization of Law*. London: Pinter.

White H.C. 2002. *Markets from Networks: Socioeconomic Models of Production*. Princeton, NJ: Princeton University Press.

Whitley R. 1992. ed. *European Business Systems: Firms and Markets in their National Contexts*. London: Sage Publications.

Whitley R. 2000. *Divergent Capitalism: The Social Structuring and Change of Business Systems*. Oxford: Oxford University Press.

Whittington R. 1988. Environmental structure and theories of strategic choice. *Journal of Management Studies* 25: 521–36.

Wishlade F. 1998a. EC Competition policy: the poor relation of EC regional policy? *European Planning Studies* 6: 573–98.

Wishlade F. 1998b. RAGS and LIPS: New Weapons in the Commission's Regional and Control Armoury. Regional and Industrial Research Paper Series No. 31. University of Strathclyde: European Policies Research Centre.

Wishlade F. 2000. Concentration of the Structural Funds and the Commission Guidelines on National Regional Aid Paper to the European Institute of Public Aministration Seminar 'Implementing the Agenda 2000 Reforms; The EU Strucutural Funds in 2000–2006' University of Strathclyde: Maastricht European Policies Research Centre.

Wishlade F., Yuill D. 2000. *EU Competition Policy and the Regions; Area designations and the New Guidelines of Regional Aid.* Presented at Regional Studies Association Conference. 'Progress, Problems and Prospects', Universite d' Aix-Marseille III, Aix-en-Provence.

Wishlade F., Yuill D. 2001. Agenda 2000 and the Targeting of EU Cohesion Policy. Mimeo, European Policies Research Centre, University of Strathclyde, Glasgow.

Zammuto R.F. 1988. Organizational adaptation: some implications of organizational ecology for strategic choice. *Journal of Management Studies* 25: 105–20.

Name Index

Subject Index